Protective Custody

Prisoner 34042

Protective Custody

Prisoner 34042

By Susan Cernyak-Spatz
Edited by Joel Shatzky with Anita Wyman

N and S Publishers

Brooklyn, N.Y.

Protective Custody Prisoner 34042
Copyright 2005 Susan Cernyak-Spatz

Cover Design: Dana Szucs

For information address:
N and S Publishers
130 Eighth Avenue Apt 5B
Brooklyn, N.Y. 11215

ISBN: 978-0-9753268-4-8
Printed in the United States of America

Table of Contents

Foreword

Susan Cernyak-Spatz, née Eckstein, was born in Vienna in 1922. In the following twenty-three years of her life she experienced many of the trials and terrors shared with her fellow Jews of middle Europe: the beginning of Nazi oppression in Berlin where she lived from 1929 to 1936; the effects of the "*Anschluss*" in Vienna where her family had relocated for, as her father mistakenly thought, "a better business climate"; and then when they were forced to move again in 1938 to Prague where she grew to young adulthood, until May, 1942 when she and her mother were deported to Theresienstadt. But the true horrors of the Nazi "Final Solution" were yet to await her in Birkenau, the woman's camp in Auschwitz where she survived her internment beginning in January, 1943, for two years. These twenty-five months of hell were followed by the "Death March" and her incarceration in Ravensbrück from which she and a group of her fellow inmates walked away to freedom.

What makes this narrative of a Holocaust survivor's experiences especially compelling is Cernyak-Spatz's compassion, tempered by detachment in her description of events, both personal and earth-shaking, that are often overwhelming for other witnesses to the logic of insanity that the Nazi called "The Final Solution." Her personal honesty about her own life and those of members of her family, and her compassion in recognizing the reasons behind the faults and short-comings of those around her given the desperate circumstances which many of them faced, reveal a woman of remarkable intelligence, insight and courage. As she says of herself in the opening part of the chapter on her experiences in Theresienstadt:

> Was it guilt that makes me block out my memories of the camp that I did not join my mother to "the East" immediately which turned out to be a death sentence? Or was it that I somehow repressed this chapter in my hegira to hell, since I was not particularly proud of my behavior there? (72)

This personal honesty, this willingness to reveal the doubts about one's integrity, which are tempting to gloss over in the selective memory which inevitably shades and limits and sometimes distorts so many of these narratives, deepens and enriches Cernyak-Spatz's insights into the psychology of Holocaust survivors. But what is also remarkable is her portrait of the life she led, not only during her three-year nightmare in concentration and death camps, but in the Hitler-plagued Berlin, Vienna and Prague prior to incarceration.

Coming from a middle-class Jewish family, Cernyak-Spatz was able to enjoy a social life that in some ways was insolated from the worst of the anti-Semitism that began to engulf the life of Jews once Hitler came to power. In her description of her grade-school routine in the mid-1930's, she reveals what still could be seen as little pockets of resistance to Nazi rule:

> I do not remember in the Chamisso Lyceum any incident of persecution. Certainly the Jewish students did not raise their arms in the Hitler salute at

student assemblies, but then neither did the teachers in the class ever use them when they entered the classroom or expected the students to do so (24).

Even in the Prague of the early war years, she and her circle of friends, among whom was the distinguished Jewish-Czech composer, Gideon Klein (1919-1944), who wrote some wonderful music while incarcerated in Theresienstadt, was able to carve out the semblance of a "normal" life. Her many friends were able to develop romantic relationships, challenge the curfews to go to parties and dances, and find ways to wall out the chaos and oppression surrounding them. Sections of this early part of the narrative resemble the life-style of the privileged Italian Jews described in Giorgio Bassani's "Garden of the Finzi-Continis." But it is when Cernyak-Spatz finally enters Theresienstadt that her story begins to reveal the frightening world that she had been able to fend off with her friends for so long.

Yet even within that world, the narrator was able to find strategies for survival particularly through the "net working" system that served her so well in Birkenau. Whether it was from the friendship with one of her circle from Prague, Lily Pohnert, or a Jewish baker in the camp who gave them extra food, Cernyak-Spatz was able to keep from falling into the despair that would later mark so many of the victims of the Nazis, the *"Muselmänner"* of Auschwitz-Birkenau who would become the willing victims of the gas chambers once their desire to live had been drained from them. When she was finally sent to the death camp, her resourcefulness was taxed by its greatest challenge: how to find a way to live in the Kingdom of Death.

The chapters on "life" in Auschwitz-Birkenau, the center of this narrative, are the most detailed, most harrowing, and most clearly and objectively described. For more than two years, from the end of January, 1943 to her evacuation from the camp in January, 1945, Cernyak-Spatz documents not only the degradation, deprivation and murderous routine of the camp, but also the courage and sacrifice of the women she met who found ways of helping and saving each other from what would have been otherwise inevitable death. She meticulously describes the process of tattooing, the "delousing," and later, when she was assigned to an *"Aussenkommando,"* the merciless "selection" of the weakest and sickest prisoners going to and returning from their ten hours of punishing physical labor for which they had been given the minimal of sustenance. Yet her own desire to survive, to find a way to overcome such inhumanity, comes through clearly even when she dismisses some of her impulses as foolhardiness. When she first was assigned her *"Kommando"* unit and was being marched out of the camp, she passed by two SS-men who were watching the procession:

> Don't ask me what prompted me to do it—was it sheer stupidity, or simply ignorance of the rules?—but I stepped out of my row of five—I was on the outside edge where the SS

men were—stood at attention and said to them: "*Melde gehorsamst; Ich bin eine Bureaukraft*" ("With your permission, I would like to report that I am an office worker"). I had addressed myself to the non-commissioned SS-man, probably figuring that the doctor would not be too interested in an office worker. For a moment the man's mouth stood open and then he laughed and wrote down my number (128-129).

She soon learned that such audacious behavior could have landed her immediately in the gas chamber, but her boldness made a lasting impression on the Nazi officer for subsequently she was given "inside jobs" that came from his recommendations. Yet, how many people, in such circumstances, would have had the presence of mind to do such a thing?

However, Cernyak-Spatz could not solely rely on her own initiative in order to survive. She needed to find a "group" of women who would look out for each other. This was obviously a way of getting through the grueling routine of the camp in which the day began before dawn and was immediately followed by the merciless *"Appell,"* the roll-call, that could go on for hours while the women shivered in the cold or baked in the sun. Many would faint and even die during the mindless counting and recounting of those able to get out of their bunks and stand up in front of the barracks. But as resourceful and physically fit as she was when she entered the camp, Cernyak-Spatz needed and found help even among the brutal camp *"blockovas,"* the women who had been on the first transports to Auschwitz and had helped establish the camp.

Once when she had become ill from typhus and would have been taken to the gas in the next selection, she was given a slim chance to recover her strength from Ilka Grün, the *blockova* of her block:

> I begged her to give me one more day resting in our block, and if after that one day I was not better, I would go to block 27 [the "hospital" from which she would be taken to the gas]. Ilka agreed and the next morning I stayed in the block. I stood

in roll call with the help of my group and then was allowed back into the block. Ilka gave me one vitamin C tablet and one aspirin. I suppose I grabbed at anything that looked like medication from the world outside; I believed it would help me. Strange to say, the miracle did happen(152-153).

Despite her illness, her will to live was strong enough, given this slender opportunity, to recover sufficiently to return to her work the following day. Through the next two years Susan Cernyak-Spatz lived through the horrors of Auschwitz-Birkenau by finding strategies for survival and eventually getting an "inside job" where at times she was an office worker, a secretary and, eventually, a member of the "elite" *Kommando* unit, *"Kanada,"* in which she sorted clothes that had been confiscated from the prisoners. She witnessed as well as experienced the system of "networking" that was run by Katja Singer and Zippi Spitzer, a personal friend, that saved the lives of many women who were in danger of turning into *Muselmänner.* She saw, understood, and has now recorded some of the many strategies of survival women in Birkenau used to defy the Nazi plan of dehumanizing them to the point that they would willingly accept their fate.

At the end of her long journey to liberation, Susan Cernyak-Spatz describes a moment of triumph when she was asked to disarm the three guards that had taken her and the rest of her group of women of the *Kanada Kommando* from Ravensbrück to the American-controlled sector of occupied Germany:

> I think that was the proudest moment of my life, as I stepped up to the old man and said: *"Hauptscharführer*, the American officer wants your gun. . . ." Reluctantly, all three gave me their guns and I carried them the few steps to the [American jeep] (240).

Finally, this seemingly endless journey for survival had ended in triumph.

Joel Shatzky

By way of Introduction to the Strange Language of the Third Reich

There are probably not too many people around who understand the word *"Schutzhäftling,"* protective custody prisoner. Like so many euphemisms introduced into the (normal) German language by the Nazis, this word had three different levels of meaning. Literally it meant that a person has been put into police custody for his or her protection. In the Nazi legal system it meant imprisonment for anti-Nazi sentiments or activity. But for the insiders in the Nazi killing machine it had only one meaning: It specifically pertained to the six million Jews who died under their regime. "Protective custody" on that level meant internment in the extermination camp with the understanding that the prisoner could be exterminated arbitrarily, not for any crime committed, not for any infraction against any rules, not for any attempt at flight, but for one reason only: because he or she was Jewish and therefore could be eliminated whenever there was an extermination action scheduled.

Strangely enough, that kind of protective custody only applied to Jews transported in a mass deportation from Nazi-occupied countries. If there happened to be a Jew caught smuggling food, or being out on the street after curfew, or for whatever offence he might have been arrested by the Gestapo, and therefore would have a file with the Gestapo, that Jew was *not* a "Protective Custody " prisoner, and could not be eliminated arbitrarily like the rest of us "protected" prisoners. He had the exclusive privilege of the right of dying his own death, i.e. he could not be sent to the gas chamber in an arbitrary selection. He was actually interned for committing a "crime." There was no reason ever given for the deaths of the millions of "protective custody" prisoners.

Chapter One

Vienna-Berlin: 1922-1936

A panoramic view of the city of Vienna makes one aware of the many church steeples surrounding the highest of them all, St. Stephen's cathedral, the beloved *"Steffel."* At the time of my birth, July 27, 1922, one of these steeples topped a small church almost at the north edge of the city, below the Kahlenberg, the famous landmark to commemorate the rout of the Turkish Army in 1683. We are in the "Silbergasse" in Döbling, then and now the 19th District of Vienna, the best neighborhood of the City to this day, the place of my birth. In 1922 the Silbergasse extended from the curve of the Billrothstrasse to the Hungerberg, then a large area of vineyards, today occupied by sumptuous villas. At the intersection of the two streets stands the Rudolfinerhaus, one the best-known hospitals of Vienna. That is where I was born.

My maternal grandparents had been living in Silbergasse 22 since well before World War I, having moved there like so many successful Viennese Jewish couples from the inner core of the city to the then almost brand new area of Döbling. My grandparents, Michael and Fanny Tauber, at the time the parents of six children, needed space and fresh air for their brood, and that they found in Döbling. Michael Tauber and his brother, Moritz, owned a galoshes factory. The two brothers had married the two Mandl sisters from Gross-Enzersdorf. At that time and until after the War it was a suburb; today it is the 23rd district of the city of Vienna. This makes my grandmother probably one of the few "real" Austrian Jewish women, in comparison with all the immigrants from the K&K[1] like Grandfather and his brother, who, as I understand it, came from Hungary.

I never heard Grandfather speak Hungarian; I don't know if he knew it. I only

---

[1]Kaiser & König Reich, the official title of the Austrian Empire territories.

know that he spoke High German with a slight Viennese inflection and forbade his children and grandchildren to use Yiddish expressions. In spite of the fact that both Grandfather and Uncle Moritz were observant, but not Orthodox Jews, it must have been important to them to appear and sound like typical Austrian upper-middle class citizens. The assimilation of the Austrian Jews extended even to intermarriage with Christians. To this day there are many aristocratic families, even in post-Hitler Vienna, whose great-grandmothers propped up their sagging aristocratic fortunes with solid Jewish merchant money.

Grandmother's brother had a large house in Gross-Enzersdorf and I remember as a teen-ager visiting his family and their beautiful gardens and orchard. The apartment in the Silbergasse had five rooms; kitchen, bath and maids' room and a veranda, and I suppose was the right size for the large family and two servants. The tutors probably didn't live in.

If I remember correctly my parents also lived there, since all Mother's brothers and sisters were living in their own residences. Father came from Poland, studied in Vienna, and served four years on the Russian and Italian front during the war. He was a dashing Lieutenant, but came from a very poor family. I never met his parents, they never left Poland. Father's sister was married to a traveling salesman in Vienna and lived in the Jewish district of Leopoldstadt. I don't know exactly how my father made a living until he and Mother moved to Berlin. He had studied law, but somehow never took his final exams. I suppose in 1928 commerce looked more promising to him than law.

My parents had joined my uncle and aunt- Mother's sister- in Berlin, to run a greeting card wholesale business, Arthur Rehn and Buck & Co, which they had bought from a Mr. Rehn, I believe. During their absence, until 1929, I stayed with my grandparents in the Silbergasse. All the windows of my grandparent's apartment, with the exception of the kitchen and the storage room, which had been their sons' bedroom when they were younger faced a beautiful backyard garden, tended by Mrs. Ferd, our janitor, whose husband had a shoe repair shop in the front of the house.

I remember a summer vacation in Bad Ischl, which to this day is one of the most exclusive resorts in Austria, and summer and winter vacations on my uncle Ricco's (Richard Tauber) estate, the *"Angerhof."* In summer there were hedges of raspberries and loads of blueberries in the forest and in the garden. My cousins, Ricco's children Kitty and Phil, and aunt Clara's children, Inge and Georg, and I took dips on hot days in an ice cold trough of water that must have been fed from a spring in the nearby mountains. And we went sledding over the fields on winter vacations. On one of these winter outings I remember, I froze my feet sledding, and I don't recall who it was who carried me into the house where my feet were stuck into a tub full of ice cold water (Not pleasant, but effective.)

to prevent frostbite. But all that happened before my parents moved to Berlin and left me with my grandparents in Vienna.

Who were my parents? Friedl Tauber, my mother, was the baby of the six Tauber family siblings. She was beautiful, and very intelligent. According to her sister Clara, she was the only one of the family who enrolled in the University of Vienna for a while. I don't know if that is true, since Aunt Clara had a tendency to brag about the family background (She really did not have to do it. There was enough to be proud of in that family without bragging.). Mother really was intelligent enough to have earned a university degree. She was high-spirited and vivacious. It must have been that *ésprit* that attracted her to Ernst Simon Eckstein, the dashing artillery lieutenant. My father loved everything artistic: music, theater, opera, operetta. Beethoven and Robert Stolz (1880-1975), the most famous popular music composer of the time, were equally his favorites. He was a wonderful dancer and my first dancing teacher. To this day I admire the photos of my father in his uniform. Life had played a funny trick on my grandfather. He, the proud citizen of Kakanien[2], had to put up with four sons-in-law of Polish descent, who, according to him, really did not fit into his assimilated social circle.

Thinking back it was clear that the romantic marriage of my parents soon lost its glamour. Mother was very demanding, and Father had not passed his law exams, therefore the proud title of "*Frau Doktor*" was denied her. In the Austrian custom to this day it is accepted that the wife of anyone with a doctor title is addressed as "*Frau Doktor.*" One of Mother's favorite sayings was: "When worries come into the door, love flies out the window." To this day I don't know whether this really was a proverb, or the result of her experiences. It described the marriage of my parents perfectly.

Both Mother and Father had their extramarital escapades. Mother always "played

---

[2] Robert Musil (1880-1942), a well-known Austrian writer, had coined this abbreviation from the designation K und K.

around" when we went on summer vacations and Father could only stay for a week, whereas she and I stayed for two or three weeks giving her opportunities to meet men unchaperoned. Dad "played around" with his secretaries. That, however, I did not find out until after his death. To the unwitting observer the marriage was probably no different from many marriages among the Jewish middleclass.

When my parents had moved to Berlin and left me with my grandparents and with Mitzi, their maid, who became—more or less--my nanny, my grandparents and Mitzi spoiled me rotten, but not to the point that they would have condoned bad behavior. I don't think I was a particularly wild or enterprising child. Most afternoons I would go walking with Mitzi over the vineyards that started not far from the Silbergasse, the vineyards of the Hungerberg, the gentle hill between the districts of Döbling and Grinzing.

I had started the first grade in the fall of 1928, and I remember being the shortest one in the class. On the first day, my cousin, George Grosser, four years my senior, came to fetch me, and present me with a *"Schultüte."* I know this isn't customary in America, but in Germany and Austria a first grader is presented with a large cornucopia filled with candy upon entering grade school for the first time. Of course the size of the cornucopia depended on the financial status of the parents. The only other thing I remember about my first year in school was that we had a male teacher. I never felt discriminated against for being Jewish, though I was probably the only Jewish child in the class.

My only bad memory of that school year was the fact that we learned to write on unlined paper with Latin script. No printing for us. When I then went into second grade in Berlin, in 1929, the writing being taught was the so-called *"Sütterlin"* (writing) script, the steeply angular writing style used at that time in the German school system. The combination of these two different writing styles resulted, to this day, in my still- illegible handwriting.

My grandparents' household was what one would call conservative in terms of religious Jewish practice. No *shaydel* (wig) for Grandmother, no *kaftan* (robe) or *payus* (side-locks) for Grandfather. I would go with him to the Saturday morning service in the Dolinagasse Temple. He was one of the Temple board members, always seated in the front on the dais, and on Saturday he would wear his top hat to Temple. He laid *tefillim* (religious articles used in prayer) every morning. The Friday night dinner was festive with candles and *challah*, and on Saturday evening grandfather made *havdallah*, the farewell prayer to the Sabbath and commemorating the beginning of the week, with the customary spice box, and the braided candle, that was extinguished in the wine to complete the ceremony.

Grandmother was a very stately woman, always dressed in black, dark-blue or brown dresses with lace at the throat, or her pearls. She wore two exquisite large diamond earrings which my cousin and I have inherited.

Grandmother could not have been more than 60 years old at that time, but remembering her stately demeanor and grooming, I can see the change of lifestyle over the past seventy years all too clearly. I can only marvel at the elegance and stateliness of these two people, who could not have been more than 60 and 68 respectively. It would be inconceivable to imagine them as people of their age would be today: physically active, dressed youthfully. But then their way of life was incredibly circumspect.

Grandfather was an elegant, white – haired man, always dressed in dark suits. I do not remember ever seeing him in a robe or in any kind of casual clothes. The only time I remember him not completely attired was in the morning, when I would see him in his long nightgown. No pajamas for my grandfather. Before his morning prayers, he would be dressed. I don't remember the rest of his routine. As far as I know, by the time I lived there, he was retired.

Every afternoon he would go to the little café, called, in Viennese dialect, the *"Tschoch,"* but don't ask me the origin or translation of the word. The place still exists on the corner of Silbergasse and the Saarpark where he would play *Tarok*, a German card game, mostly played by men. I never learned whom he played with, because, of course, I was not allowed into the café: no place for a child. Instead, my realm was the Saarpark, the fairly big park with the large chestnut trees shading the big sandbox close to the entrance from the Silbergasse. When I returned there in 1973 nothing had changed, except the chestnut trees were larger.

But by then none of the familiar stores along our side of the Silbergasse were there anymore. Not the grocery store, presided over by the genial "Herr Lambert," not the candy store, owned by "Herr Fuernkranz" who turned out to be quite a Nazi, or the electric appliance and repair shop belonging to "Herr Pollacek." Like most of Vienna's Jews, he probably was deported either to Theresienstadt and/or to Auschwitz.

I can't remember whether it was Father or Mother who came to fetch me from Vienna in 1929, but I am sure I did not travel alone. I also am not sure how hard it was to say goodbye to Grandfather and Grandmother. However, I knew we would see them at least once a year, since the whole family always congregated at the grandparents' house on Passover.

That winter in Berlin was probably the coldest that I can recall. We lived in rented rooms in the Sächsische Strasse, close to the Fehrbelliner Platz. I can still remember one very cold day that winter, when I suppose the central heating was out, or perhaps there were coal stoves and not enough coal. But I recall how Mother, the maid, and I had put a board across the bathtub and that is where we ate our lunch, the only warm place in the three rooms we rented there. Probably the little gas stove in the bathroom kept that spot warmer than the rest of the apartment.

In the summer of 1929 we moved to a four-room apartment with kitchen and maids' room in a brand-new apartment house on the Tempelhofer Weg in Friedenau. It was the road to the Tempelhof airport. Within several blocks our building was the only one on our side of the street, and the grade school across the street was the other one. I was registered into the second grade in that school. I never thought later that I would ever see anyone again from that period of my life.

But life can play strange tricks. In 1999, on my yearly lecture series in Heidelberg, sponsored by the Friedrich Ebert *Gedenkstätte*, I gave a lecture in Weinheim, a little town close to Heidelberg. The lecture was reviewed in the Weinheim newspaper, and I suppose I must have mentioned my maiden name, because shortly thereafter I received a call from a Mrs. Hildegard Close. She remembered having been in the second grade with me, and even described the birthday party that she had been invited to at our apartment. She had been terribly impressed with the white apron and cap of the maid. As modern as the building was, there was nevertheless a rear courtyard with stables for draft horses that were housed there. These were Clydesdales, and they were pretty scary when they sometimes reared up against their drivers.

Another scary memory of my life in Berlin which I remember to this day was that once a man, probably when I crossed the street from school to the house, tried to persuade me to go with him, but I ran as fast as I could into the house because it had been drilled over and over again into my head: "Never talk to or go anywhere with a stranger." I even remember the names of my best girl friends in school although Hilde Close was not one of them. Their names were Gisela Madeja and Ingeborg Katschinski. Ingeborg might have been Jewish. At that time that never entered anyone's mind. Everyone knew that I did not have a Christmas tree, and I was always invited to the so-called "plundering of the tree" on January 6th. The trees at that time were decorated with cookies and candies and confectionary.

The girls lived in the public housing in the Gothenstrasse, which was the next cross street after mine from the Tempelhofer Weg. I loved to play with them in the grass and flower-covered inner courtyards of the public housing complex. I never knew what their parents did for a living, I suspect they were small retail merchants, or office workers. They did not belong to my parents' circle of friends.

In 1932 I was admitted into the Chamisso Lyceum (girl's high school). At that time, in Germany, grade school, or as it was called, *Volksschule,* consisted of 10 grades, and one could receive ten years of schooling for free. However, if one had ambitions for one's child, one would enroll him or her after the fourth grade in the gymnasium, or the lyceum respectively. These were the institutions that prepared students for higher education and they were semi-private; there were fees and the books had to be paid for by the parents.

These educational institutions, after eight years, would lead to the so-called *abitur* or *matura* certification as it was called in Austria. The education one received in these institutions entitled a student, after passing the *abitur* successfully, to enter the university. To this day the four years of college, required for entry to an American university, do not exist in Europe.

The wholesale greeting card company my father partially owned must have succeeded beyond expectations, because the principal owners, my Mother's sister and brother-in-law, Uncle Siegfried and Aunt Paula, had moved from their apartment in Friedenau, not a particularly desirable neighborhood, to the Münchnerstrasse, near the Bayerische Platz, one of the best neighborhoods in Berlin. Since Mother never could stand to be outdone by her sister, we, too, had moved to that area, in the Bambergerstrasse. Though the house we moved into had been built in 1915, it had central heating, hot and cold water, an elevator and a concierge. The KaDeWe, the most elegant department store in Berlin, was about 20 minutes away on foot, and next to that street was the Kurfürstendamm, the most elegant street after "Unter den Linden." In short, we now lived at the right address.

For my education at age 10, I was sent to the closest lyceum with the best reputation for providing a classic education, which was the Chamisso Lyceum on Barbarossa Square. My homeroom teacher was Fräulein von Hauff, a petite, elegant woman, who was also our French teacher. I can still recite some of the lines from some of LaFontaine's famous fables: *"Maitre corbeau sur un arbre perché, tenait en son becque un fromage...."* Any French accent I have today came from Madame von Hauff. Her accent was flawless and she insisted on correct pronunciation.

Until 1933 my cousin, Hannelore, and I walked together to school. I would come by her house to pick her up and we were on our way. Shortly after Hitler's arrival Hannelore and her parents moved to Prague. Why my father stayed behind I'll never know. I suspect it had to do with bringing most of my uncle's movable property to Prague.

I found two good friends in the lyceum very shortly after I entered, Herta Dunsig and Dita Raetz-Waldenburg. If I remember correctly, the fathers of both girls were either in the SA or the SS, but it seems no one was bothered by that. Later on I have often wondered why I was so completely accepted by Herta's as well as Dita's parents. This might have something to do with Dr.Goebbels dictum: "...every German knows some very nice and decent Jews. If we take all of them into consideration we will never solve the Jewish problem." We visited back and forth and were close friends. Herta and I went to the same ballet school since I was a dedicated dancer and saw myself as a prima ballerina of the future.

In my class there were two other Jewish girls, Hanni and Ruth. Hanni came from the same middle class as I did. Ruth's father was a tailor, one of the few Jewish craftsmen I ever knew. Of course we had some Jewish workers in our warehouse and office but they lived on the north side of Berlin, which seemed to be the lower class Jewish neighborhood. Ruth was the best gymnast in our class, better than any of the blonde valkyries. When they had to eliminate her from competition, because she was Jewish, the team did not win any more prizes as they had when Ruth was in the group.

I can only imagine that this happened because the school did not want to have a Jewish-looking athlete in the competition. After all, Jews were not supposed to be athletes, according to the German propaganda. I was in the Chamisso Lyceum until the third grade, the Quarta, and was one of the good students, thanks to my father's urging, who always said "To be equal as a Jew we have to be better."

In the summer of 1933 I encountered the first Nazi youth groups I'd ever seen. We were in Kolberg on the Baltic Sea, a well-known summer resort. I remember walking with our maid, and a marching band of either Hitler Youth or Pimpfe, that was the younger group, something on the order of Cub Scouts, came down the street. I remember being envious that I could not belong to and cheer the group. Many years later I read Ionescu's "Rhinoceros" and recalled what the author said about the impetus for the play. It seemed he was in Germany in the 30's and like myself encountered one of the marching bands with flags and music, parading through a cheering crowd with their arms upraised in the Hitler salute. Ionescu said that he had to hold his arm down to prevent himself from following the motions of the crowd. He also wanted to belong. That moment was the origin of "Rhinoceros."

Many times, when I hear survivors from Berlin talk about how they were persecuted and discriminated against during the early years of the Hitler regime, I wonder whether or not my parents protected me from any knowledge of what was going on, or whether the district we lived in simply was not populated by rabid fanatics. I do not remember in the Chamisso Lyceum any incident of persecution. Certainly the Jewish students did not raise their arms in the Hitler salute at student assemblies, but then neither did the teachers in class ever use them when they entered the classroom, or expected the students to do so.

I was in the Chamisso Lyceum until 1935 and I do not know whether at that time my parents were asked to remove me, or whether they decided I should go to a Jewish school. But at the beginning of that school year, I was transferred to Miss Zickel's private school in the Kufsteiner Strasse, near our house. It was a very exclusive private school that had existed long before the advent of Hitler and of course now flourished since the Jewish enrollment increased considerably due to their expulsion from the public schools.[3] The school became so crowded that it was moved from the two floors in the apartment house where it had been founded to an old school building in Friedenau.

---

[3] In September, 1935, Hitler's government established the Nuremberg Laws which, among other provisions, forbade the attendance of Jewish students in public schools and universities.

The "Bayrische Platz," our neighborhood, was one of the best in the city, outside of the Tiergarten, or the Grunewald, where the villas of the wealthy families stood. Father would take the subway every morning to go to his office in the north of Berlin. Sometimes, on Saturdays, when he worked only half days, he would take me with him to the office and it was my greatest joy to help prepare the greeting card assortments that were arranged to fill the orders. I presume Mother was bored with doing nothing, because I remember she was an excellent bridge player and put this knowledge to use, running a bridge salon in the elegant KaDeWe, located on Tauenziehn Strasse.

The one thing my parents had in common aside from me was their very active social life, attending theatres, concerts and balls. Mother told me once how she had been at the opening night of Ferenc Molnar's *Lilliom* in Berlin, starring the then famous film star, Hans Albers (1891-1960).

By the end of 1936, Father, whose business had not been bothered in any way due to his Polish citizenship, decided it was time to transfer it to a politically safer location. He had had that protection because at that time Poland was a sovereign state and foreign citizens, whether Jewish or not, did not come under the jurisdiction of the Third Reich. Why at this point he decided to transfer the business to Vienna, in view of the apparent political ambitions of Hitler regarding Austria, I will never understand. But then I was "the child" and was never asked or consulted about anything. In the end my inbred lack of assertiveness brought me into Theresienstadt and Auschwitz. It might sound strange today that I claim submission to the decisions of my parents, and I can only assume that it must have been the subsequent fight for survival that hardened me to the point of aggressiveness. I was a meek, very obedient child, and I think that to the day I saw her the last time in Theresienstadt, my mother had never heard me say NO to any of her decisions.

Obedience was a given, even if you boiled inside.

Our religious life in Berlin was that of the average middle-class assimilated Jewish family. We were still Jewish enough to have a somewhat festive dinner on Friday nights with the candle lighting and the prayers over bread and wine. Every so often we would even go to temple on Friday night. Of course we attended on the High Holidays, i.e. everybody went on Rosh HaShana. And the adults went on Yom Kippur since they would stay in Temple all day.

I remember when I was in second or third grade, being home alone with the maid, while my parents were in Temple for Yom Kippur. I was standing at the bay window and looked out over the deserted street. There was not much traffic on Tempelhofer Weg: a few beer carts, not many autos. I was asking the Lord for forgiveness for my sins, which I knew we were supposed to do on Yom Kippur. I am not quite sure for what sins I tried to atone.

While living in the west end of Berlin, on Bamberger Strasse, we went to the newest and most reformed synagogue in Berlin, the Prinzregentenstrasse synagogue. The rabbi of that synagogue was Dr. Joachim Prinz (1902-1988) who made quite a name for himself in America as a rabbi of Temple B'nai Abraham in Newark, N.J. after leaving Germany in 1937. He became a noted Civil Rights activist and participated in the Civil Rights March on Washington in 1963.

My father was more of a nationalist and Zionist than a religious Jew, very well informed about modern Jewish history, from about the nineteenth century on, including the history of Zionism. To this day I cannot understand why he, such an ardent Zionist, did not immigrate to Palestine when Hitler came to power. I suspect Mother was not particularly attracted to sand and heat and a pioneering lifestyle, and Father, of course, deferred to her wishes.

The years in Berlin I remember actually as the only normal ones of my adolescence.

Sunday morning walks with Father and/or Mother to the Schöneberger municipal park, near the Schöneberger City Hall; going on weekends to the market on the Rathaus Square with Mother; going on walks, or to the movies, or to cafés with the group of young Jewish people my age. We also enjoyed eating ice cream in the little ice cream parlor at the corner of the Kufsteiner and Grunewaldstrasse. There was no such thing as thinking about any sexual escapades. We always went in groups, no single dating.

I suppose we knew about political events, but simply refused to be affected by them. I am sure the parents of our group were making arrangements to leave for overseas; at least I hope they had more sense than my parents. We were the only family in my circle of friends who went to Vienna, as did my uncle and aunt, my Mother's sister, Paula, who had previously moved to Prague in 1933. The branch of the greeting card company in Vienna was expanded and we all arrived there together in 1936.

Chapter Two
Vienna: 1936-1938

I will never know what prompted my parents to make this decision at that particular time rather than emigrate from Europe entirely. Hitler had made numerous remarks in his speeches about Austria actually belonging to the greater German Reich, if not immediately, then soon. The whole world was holding its collective breath about the madman's next move. German Jews stood in line for visas to emigrate overseas, anywhere overseas, and my parents invested good money to move to Vienna and renovate the apartment of my grandmother, Silbergasse 22, from top to bottom, and modernize it according to Mother's taste. I still suspect that this move was Mother's decision. She did not want to have to pay the so-called

"*Reichfluchtsteuer,*"[1] the horrendous tax Jews had to pay, if they actually emigrated. At that time my father, having Polish citizenship, probably would not have had to pay that tax at all. Perhaps Mother feared possible deprivation in her lifestyle if she started somewhere from scratch, especially if it would have been Palestine, where living conditions would have been primitive and difficult and the challenge of learning an entirely new language tremendous.

The *fait accompli* was that we arrived in Vienna, in the winter of 1936. I remember that my aunt Helen took me for a skiing vacation on the Semmering, a very fashionable summer and winter resort near Vienna, so that I would be out of Mother's hair while she redecorated the apartment. The branch office of Arthur Rehn & Co in Vienna, in the meantime having been

---

[1] On December 8, 1931, more than a year before Hitler came to power, the Weimar Government instituted a law to discourage capital flight and emigration during the Depression. Assets of more than 200,000 marks were taxed at a rate of 25%. On May 18, 1934, under the Nazi regime, the law was renewed with a limit of 50,000 marks or an income of 20,000 marks with the same 25% tax rate.

renamed *Reproducta,* was now expanded, located in the Nussdorferstrasse 14, a fairly large apartment house that Uncle Siegfried and Aunt Paula had bought. They had the building renovated in order to have a large apartment on the first floor for themselves, a small apartment for Grandmother, and the office and warehouse in the back of the building. A branch of the Delka shoe company was located in the house on the main floor. There was a lovely garden, almost a small park, in the back. Since we all had lived in apartments all our lives, this garden, as part of the property, was thoroughly enjoyed by everyone in the family.

Mother redecorated the apartment as if we were ready to settle there for the rest of our lives. I presume she really convinced herself that her future in Vienna was protected from Hitler's plans. Life took on its usual routine; I was registered into the Döblinger women's gymnasium, on the Billrothstrasse. Today the building is gone; there is some other school there. My school had the dubious honor of having been the one that Hedy Lamarr (1914-2000, née Hedwig Eva Marie Kiesler; notable Hollywood actress and inventor of wireless technology) was expelled from for unseemly behavior with a professor named Lohner. Like with any change of schools, it was wrenching for me, in that one had to start making new friends in a class that had been together from practically the first grade of the gymnasium.

The summer of 1937, Mother, my cousin Hella, and I went to Balaton Almadi, a small resort on the Plattensee in Hungary. Father, as usual, did not come with us. We had always taken summer vacations abroad, in the Dolomites, in the Erzgebirge, the Riesengebirge, the Austrian Alps. Actually Almadi was the first summer vacation that was not in the mountains and it was also the last normal summer vacation of my youth. That winter there were a lot of student dances. Every gymnasium and many student organizations would give balls. My first evening gowns were made by the faithful Frau Hansi, the house seamstress, who would come for a day or two with patterns and her sewing machine. Not even we girls, i.e. Inge, aunt Clara's daughter and Hannelore, aunt Paula's daughter, even though being only 15, would wear any ready-made clothes. Everyone had her seamstress, Father his tailor, and Mother even a *modiste*, a hat-maker. Thus in my world even hats were made to order. I remember the little *modiste* was in the Silbergasse, a few blocks up from our house.

However, my teenage years, which should have been my most happy, were rather tame. It was only in 1937 that I had my first date, and on that date my first French kiss from a boy who was about to graduate from the gymnasium, so he must have been close to 19. His name was Benno Gerstenhaber. I wonder if he is still alive.

In March 1938, the *Anschluss*, Hitler's annexation of Austria, changed our lives. In the early years after the Second World War, the Austrians tried to get sympathy from other countries for having been the first country overrun, so to speak, by Hitler, his "first 'victims.'" What was not widely known, but became common knowledge later, was that that excuse was promoted by the Allies. It seems that the Russian menace already at that time was recognized as threatening to Western Europe. About the time of Churchill's "Iron Curtain" speech in Fulton, Missouri in 1946, it was decided by the Western Allies to have a neutral buffer state between the threatening Eastern bloc and the West. Austria seemed to be ideally located, but one could not very well have a former Axis member, one of Hitler's proudest possessions, be an ally of the victorious nations. So Austria was simply declared not Hitler's ally, which it was, but Hitler's "victim," which it decidedly was not. When the German Army marched into Austria in March of 1938, they were drowned in seas of flowers and enthusiasm.

Not until 1988 did the Austrians who were there at the *Anschluss* have to admit their guilt when the whole subterfuge was acknowleged and they revealed their complicity in Hitler's take over. It was then over forty years later that exhibitions were publicly shown of the newsreel of the *Anschluss*, as well as the headlines from newspapers, full of fervent vows of allegiance to the Führer by people who after the War pretended to have been victimized, like the famous conductor Herbert von Karajan (1908-1989) as well as Paul Hörbiger (1895-1981), Austria's favorite film actor (noted by American audiences as the porter in "The Third Man" (1949)), and many others. And it was deserved guilt, because during the time of my incarceration in Birkenau, the highest positions in the camp, such as the head matron and the camp leader, and many other thoroughly despicable characters, were Austrians. A post-war "joke" goes: the Germans were good Nazis, but poor anti-Semites; the Austrians were poor Nazis, but very good anti-Semites. Contrary to revised post-war history, not only did the Austrians receive the Nazis with great joy and enthusiasm, they also went to work on anti-

Semitic excesses with a fervor that had not been seen in the Reich itself since the Nazis took power in 1933.

There is much literature about the initial days of the Hitler occupation. The gleeful anti-Semitism displayed by the population found its outlet in vicious delights, such as making Jews scrub the sidewalks, which had been covered with Schuschnigg propaganda, prior to the incursion (Kurt von Schuschnigg (1897-1977) Austrian Premier prior to the *Anschluss*). They would stop anyone who even in the least looked Jewish, without asking for identification, and force him or her to do these demeaning activities. They called these Jews in the street *"A-raber."* *"Raben"* is the Austrian dialect for *"reiben"* meaning "to scrub." They would take others into the military barracks in town and have them clean the latrines with toothbrushes. They would stop men with beards if they looked Jewish, and would cut, or even rip, the beards off them in the street. I did not see these things, but heard of them and then saw them in the

1938 newsreels shown in the 1988 exhibit in the Vienna City Hall.

My mother would not let me go into town, where these incidents occurred. In our neighborhood in Döbling, things like that did not happen. I suppose the lower classes, participating in these "games," did not dare to come into the upper-class neighborhoods. It could have been a matter of upbringing. Upper-class Austrians were probably just as anti-Semitic, but they they did not take to the streets. They did not have to. They acquired all the expropriated properties of the Jews. One of the reasons why Austrian Jewish emigration began immediately and urgently after *Anschluss* was just that climate. In Germany, emigration had until that time been at a steady pace, but not in a flood as in Austria.

My father had been at that time in Prague in our office there. He and my uncle had left before March 11, the date on which *Anschluss* officially occurred. To this day I do not know how it was that my aunt and her daughter managed to leave Vienna practically the day of the Nazi arrival, and my mother and I stayed there. If I wanted to be suspicious, I would have to think that it was again a matter of my mother not wanting to leave anything behind, like her jewelry and the apartment. But the Gestapo came, in the beginning of May, and took both.

Mother blamed a new maid we had for setting the Gestapo on our trail, but I am not sure. Mother had accused her of stealing, and at that point all it took for an Aryan to denounce a Jew and have his property confiscated was to have any kind of flimsy accusation. We will never know: all the participants, except me, are dead. In any case, after that episode we of course received our exit visas: we were foreign nationals after all. This was my first flight. Two little suitcases in hand, we flew to Prague. It can be assumed with certainty that the next day a high-ranking Gestapo or SS member walked into our apartment and began his life among our clothes, china, silver, furniture, and even the food in the pantry.

Chapter Three
Prague: 1938-1942

Zlata Praha, golden Prague. Strange, I can rarely remember my dreams, but whenever I dream of a city, I seem to remember that dream, and most of the time the city is Prague. Not that all my memories of the city were necessarily wonderful; on the contrary, it was the town where we were refugees. I don't know what it was that kept me enthralled with Prague: was it its beauty or was it the experience of first love in that city that made it so memorable? All of the participants in that magic are dead, so I'll never know. Pips Schlesinger, my love, would be 84 years old by now. Memory keeps old loves young and new it seems.

Mother and I arrived in Prague an hour after leaving Vienna behind. My father picked us up from the airport in Ruzyn, and we went into the city by taxi. We crossed the Moldau by the

Smeruv Bridge, the one leading directly into the Revolucni Trida, one of the main streets, which ended at the Prasna Brana (The Powder Tower), one of the many landmarks of Prague.

The taxi stopped at Hradebni 11, a street running parallel to the Revolucni. All the streets ended at the Quai, a broad promenade along the river. The house in Hradebni 11 was a combination office and small apartment house, the apartments not being larger than containing two bedrooms at the most with a bathroom and a small area with a sink for cooking. The apartments were meant for out-of-towners who had their business in the building and used it as a sort of company apartment. In May of 1938 the apartments were filled with Austrian and German refugees who had all left their large apartments, just as we had, with everything in them behind, and who were grateful for the shelter of the small flats. It could have been much worse. Not all housing that was affordable for refugees in this old city had that much modern comfort.

My uncle had rented the apartment in 1936, when the office in Vienna was established, so that he would not have to stay at a hotel when he visited the Prague branch and would be in the same building, which took care of any transportation problems in the city. The office was on the first floor of Hradebni 11, and was now called Reproducta. The apartment was very efficient for one person to spend a few days there, but it was tight quarters for the three of us on a more-or-less permanent basis.

Shortly after arriving in Prague I came down with a severe case of strep throat. The threat of infection for my parents was serious in this small apartment so my cousin who lived in Prague, Ruth, my uncle Siegfried's daughter from his first marriage, offered to keep me at her house. She lived in the so-called New City of Prague, in a street called Podskalska, and had an extra bedroom. It was really a sacrifice for Ruth to take me in, since she had a little girl whose room I occupied and she had to keep the little one strictly away from me. It took almost until July for me to recuperate.

Living in the small apartment with my parents was not the most comfortable since the one large room we had got quite hot. After getting well and returning to my parents, I worked part time for Reproducta doing their German correspondence. I remember that we still did quite a bit of business with Nazi Germany. Obviously the political situation did not interfere with business; an axiom that is eternal and universal. One thinks of the active German–American collaboration during the War in arms and technology. For example, IBM collaborated with Germany in the development of the Hollerith punch card machine that enabled the Nazis to organize the data base in order to implement the Holocaust systematically.[1]

---

[1] See Edwin Black. IBM and the Holocaust; the Strategic Alliance Between Nazi Germany and America's Most Powerful Corporation. New York: Crown Publishers, 2001. It details the collaboration between the Hollerith Maschinen Gesellschaft m.b.H. and the IBM Corp. during the entire War.

While I was staying at her house, I had asked my cousin whether there was a place to go swimming in a suitable neighborhood that I could reach on foot or by trolley. She told me about the Manes swimming pool. It was not actually a pool, but decks below the café Manes on the banks of the Moldau. Yes, we swam in the Moldau River that ran through Prague and it was clean and safe to bathe in. There I made my first contacts with young Jewish people who were all my age, and being of the young Jewish Prague elite, all spoke fluent German. It was strange how strongly the German language and culture pervaded the Jewish population of Prague. We did have one non-Jew in our group, Toni Bartel, our "token goy," a painter. He was older than most of us, and worked as a designer and graphic artist for Paramount Pictures. I fell desperately in love with him, but for him I was just little Susi: I was all of 16 years old.

I made some of my best friends in that group, like Emmy Müllerova, a native Prague girl, and her cousin Nina. Nina's father was a well-known attorney, and Emmy's father worked in an office. Emmy did survive the war in Israel, but died about 12 or so years ago. Life did not deal with her kindly after having attained her freedom. She had gone to Israel with one of the illegal transports that took ships down the Danube through the black sea. She married a man who treated her badly and her son, influenced by the father, was just as rotten to her. Her cousin Nina died in Auschwitz, but Nina's sister, Melli, survived and lives in Washington DC. These were the first friends I made in Prague.

In the apartment house in the Hradebni, two brothers also resided; Franta and Rudla Löwy from Pilsen. Both worked in Prague: Rudla worked at a shipping firm that our company did business with, but I don't remember where Franta worked. Rudla asked my father if he could invite me to a 5 o'clock tea. It was my first date in Prague, and of course, my mother insisted on going along as a chaperone.

Life became somewhat normal in Prague, in spite of living in the one- bedroom flat with Mother and Father. We went to the five o'clock teas, we went swimming, we flirted, and it was around that time that I got the first slap in the face from my father, when, one night, I came home later than my curfew. I don't remember if it was a date with Rudla, or with someone else, but it was the first and last time I was slapped.

My parents became acquainted with the many Viennese immigrants in the various coffeehouses in the center of the city. I presume everyone discussed the political situation and the future possibilities. In the Fall of 1938 anyone with eyes in his head had to see what was coming. The Czech army had been mobilized. Rudla as a lieutenant in the reserves was of course called up. He looked splendid in his uniform. Strangely enough I don't remember hearing anything about Crystal Night, when during the pogrom on November 9, 1938, mobs destroyed Jewish shops and synagogues throughout Germany and killed many people.

Did I suppress that memory, or perhaps I did not bother to read the Czech papers, or could not read them yet? I don't know. But I remember nothing about it at that time.

However, March 14, 1939 I remember only too well, when the Austrian drama repeated itself in Prague and the German army invaded Czechoslovakia and declared it a "Protectorate." But this time there was no enthusiastic reception as in Vienna, no flowers thrown, no arms raised. Sad faces, tears and suppressed curses. It did, however, not take long until a pro-Nazi figure emerged to do the bidding of the Third Reich: a former General by the name of Rudolf Gajda, who urged the Prague population to collaborate with the conqueror. Many of them complied. The name of the group was *"Vlajka"* which means "flag." Ironically, in spite of Gajda's enthusiasm for the Nazis, his own good-looking Aryan son was among our group of Jewish young people. In 1939 there were no prohibitions against social functions by Jews.

Before the actual prohibitions started in 1941 the very first requirement was that all the Jews had to register with the German authorities after the War broke out. It was at that time that the Nazis began their campaign of systematic robbery of Jewish property that allowed them to finance the War. Jewelry, furs, electric appliances anything that looked like it could be useful, was confiscated. Mother and I did not have many things to surrender, as far as appliances were concerned. I believe we kept our little radio. And I kept a little fur bolero. The jewelry had been confiscated in Vienna.

Some time during 1939, after the outbreak of the War, we had to move out from Hradebni 11. Before that time, it must have been about July or August 1939, my father, who had finally made up his mind, after the German occupation, that we had to go to the West and possibly overseas, made arrangements for all of us to cross the Polish-Czech border illegally. The Poles at that time had closed their borders to the Czech area, I presume because of the

German occupation. When all the arrangements were complete for our departure, my mother demurred, saying to my father: "You go, and if you succeed in crossing the border, the child and I will follow. As it is, it is too dangerous for all of us to go." This rationale, of course, was totally spurious, because if Father had not succeeded he would be either dead or incarcerated by the Nazis, and we would have been arrested for being members of his family. But Father, as usual, followed Mother's request and left by himself. He left, however, on August 31, 1939, and as they say, the rest is history: history that began on September 1, 1939 with the German invasion of Poland. Father must have managed to get out of Poland on one of the last planes leaving before the border was sealed; Mother and I were trapped.

I can't help believing that this was her excuse not to leave Prague, because she probably was already emotionally involved with Rudi Guth, a former industrialist, and did not want to leave him. It seems possible that she was so madly in love with him that she simply did not think about me and the dangers I would also face. After all, I was just a young girl and belonged with my mother; that must have been her reasoning. Such reasoning cost her her life and me two years in Birkenau.

Shortly after Father left, we had to move from the Hradebni to an apartment we shared with another Jewish mother and daughter, who I presume were in the same tight financial situation as we were. The Germans had blocked all Jewish bank accounts, and only allowed the owners a small amount monthly to draw from the account.

The left side of the street on Revolucni Trida consisted of modern blocks of flats. There, in one of these houses, two doors north of the Café National, we found an apartment to share with Ms. Schiller, and her daughter Kitty. I presume Mother knew why Ms. Schiller was alone with her daughter. It could have been the same reason as in our case. Mother never informed me, and Kitty and I never talked about it. The apartment consisted of two bedrooms, a bath, and a small cooking nook.

Kitty Schiller belonged to the young Prague Jewish elite, such as Gaby Meislova, Lisa Roubicek, Jirka Taussig, Zappi Schifferes, who later married Lisa's brother Walter, Peter Holub, George Landesmann and a few others whose name I have forgotten. Toni Bartel still belonged to the group at that time, though not quite "officially." Sometimes our former Manes group and the elite group mixed in social events, such as I remember in 1940.

A young member of our group, Max Eisler, a journalist and a very witty and intelligent writer, and Gideon Klein, the composer who later became famous in Theresienstadt, and who was killed in Auschwitz, wrote a musical in the model of Hollywood musicals. Lisa Roubicek, or rather her mother, let us use their apartment. I don't know how come they still had a big apartment on the Letna, a very exclusive neighborhood of Prague. It was a big place, five-six rooms, kitchen and baths. The living room was separated from the small dining room with a sliding door.

We used the dining room as the stage and the sliding door as the curtain and produced "*Liebe ohne Liebe*," ("Love without Love") our musical. I still remember the main melody. Gideon, the classical composer, had written a "swinging" operetta, and probably not a note of it has been recorded. He accompanied us on the piano, and who would have thought that we were being accompanied by one of the greatest composers of modern Europe.

Some of my friends, like Lisa and Zappi and Walter and George, survived, but not many. Two members of our group were the Selig brothers, Wolfi and Honza. The Selig family was one of the best known Jewish bankers of Prague, owning a big banking firm located on the "Graben." Wolfi had married Lisa Wolf, one of my colleagues in my retraining gymnastic course, that was run by Fredy Hirsch. At that time in Prague, and probably in other German-occupied countries, where Jews were thinking of emigrating, the ORT organization, a Jewish organization dedicated at the time to retraining Jews, sponsored among other courses a gymnastic-teacher course. Both brothers were deported to Theresienstadt and though Wolfi was AK-I, the supposedly protected Pioneer Transport, they both were sent to Auschwitz to die there.

As soon as the *"Blitzkrieg"* was over, my Mother and I lost our foreign citizen status, since Poland now belonged to Hitler, and we became stateless. That meant that we were merely tolerated by the Czech authorities. We had to report every month to the police to renew our residence permit. Since Mother never learned a word of Czech, it became my task to do all the shopping and whatever needed to be negotiated in the vernacular. Thanks to my talent for learning languages easily (by then I could speak German, English and French as well), I had picked up enough Czech between 1938 and the 1939 German occupation to make myself understood, because at that time it was rather dangerous to speak German.

The Czechs between 1938, when we arrived in Prague, and 1939, at the time of the German occupation, were militantly anti-German. My pronunciation of Czech had become almost accent-free by then. That was also one of the talents that helped me survive Birkenau, where the lingua franca was Slovak and also Polish. I managed to learn Polish rather quickly, since all Slavic languages are very much alike.

By now our financial situation had become quite precarious, since all Jewish accounts were frozen and we were allowed to take only 1500 Crowns (a crown is worth $.05 in today's currency) from the bank. That made life very difficult.

Our group of friends was in constant flux. From time to time one or the other managed to get permission to leave with a visa to an unoccupied country. New people joined the group. I remember particularly a young

Viennese, a cousin of the writer Annemarie Selinko (1914-1986) author of "Desirée" one of the best-selling novels of the pre-war era. Hans was tall, dark-haired and gorgeous, but I could not return his ardent feelings. Many years later I saw him in Israel. He still was tall and dark-haired, but a grenade in the 1948 War had totally disfigured him. Many operations later he was still a frightening sight.

He had left Prague with one of the illegal transports to Palestine arranged by Herr Mandler's travel agency between 1940 and 1941. This travel agency was mainly occupied with arranging for passage for Jewish youngsters to Palestine. It was rumored that Mandler had some kind of arrangement with the Nazis and had paid them off to facilitate the exit and transit visas for the travelers. If that was so, he should have been recommended, but he played politics, with his ability to choose who would go in one of his transports and who would be rejected. It all depended on how much one could pay. When it came Mandler's turn to be deported, he was given privileged status in Theresienstadt and was not sent on to Auschwitz.

I had worked in that agency for a while in 1941, because I had hoped that I could get the opportunity to join one of the transports for less money than Mandler asked, since I worked for him. But of course Mother would not hear of it. When he heard my story after the war in Israel, Hans Selinko said: "How terrible to think that you could have been spared all that if your Mother would have let you go with the transport."

That was not the only proof of my Mother's egotism. Many years later my cousin Inge, who had been sent by her parents to Brussels to my uncle, and had managed to immigrate to America before Belgium was occupied, told me of the many phone calls that had been made to my mother by my father and all of the family there, to let at least me come to Brussels, if she refused to come. They had a visa for me and everything was arranged. But

Mother refused to let me go, and never told me of any of these phone calls during her lifetime.

At about that time in the summer of 1940 I met my first great love, Pips Schlesinger. His name was Peppo,--Josef--, but everyone called him Pips. We met in a little nightclub on the Vinohradska that had become a sort of "in" place for Jewish young people. It later was one of the few restaurants permitted for Jews to frequent. There was a coffeehouse on the main floor and a nightclub in the basement. That was the arrangement in quite a few cafés. He had asked me to dance and since we danced well together, we danced most of that evening, and from then on we saw each other frequently. At that point we just dated, nothing more. He was a painter and designer and lived together with another art student, a Montenegriner named Ahmed. Pips' mother also lived in Prague, but separately. His father, a textile engineer who was working in Kovno, (Lithuania), was trying to get his family visas to join him.

Pips was multitalented: he was very musical as well as artistic. His paintings of Prague's Mala Strana, the district below the Hradschin, the castle hill, were little jewels. He sold some of them. He sketched me many times, and I wish I had some of the sketches. We went for a lot of walks in Prague's romantic neighborhoods that had remained unaltered since the middle ages, and parks with large majestic trees hundreds of years old. Pips loved to recite poetry. We both loved Rainer Maria Rilke's (1875-1926) "Cornet," a long elegy written in 1899 by the great German-Czech poet which is in memory of an ancestor who had lived two hundred and fifty years before; we could recite pages of it by heart.

I finally did sleep with Pips, after many months, and it originally was almost an act of revenge. I caught my Mother one day in bed with Rudi Guth, the man for whom she had let my father leave without us. And to spite her, who was very concerned that I keep my innocence for a possible advantageous marriage, I started my affair with Pips. I was lucky that he was such a decent young man, that he really loved me, and did not just want me in his bed. But then times were different. In our circles there were no "one night stands." I really did love him; however, to be truthful, the thought of defying my Mother made the decision considerably easier.

Finally, sometime in the middle of 1941, Pips' father managed to get a visa for his family. Until the time Pips left we belonged to a group of young people who led an almost defiant life. In spite of restrictions on traveling and movement, we, the *"Haselbacher"* (that is what we called ourselves), went dancing in our little bar, and traveled in Fall, Winter and Spring to Hradesovice, a small town not far from Prague, where for the right money, the proprietors of two little hotels were willing to let us Jews stay, to wander, ski and enjoy ourselves. The room rental could not have been very much since none of us had any extra money to spend, due to the fact that our families' accounts had been frozen. With the exception of two men, Bruno, a heavy-set fellow, who seemed to have unlimited amounts of money, and Honza, in whose flat we all spent many a night playing bridge and listening to the radio and drinking, none of us had much money to spend.

By that time there was already a curfew for Jews from 8 p.m. to 8 a.m., and thus we were always facing the possibility of being caught and arrested. I wonder, did we just not want to face reality, or did we think that nothing terrible would happen if we were found violating these restrictions? Little did we realize that such infractions would have landed us all in a concentration camp or possibly an extermination camp. After Pips left I worked in Mandler's travel agency as I mentioned before. But due to my Mother's refusal, the Palestinian avenue of escape was closed, as well as any future I might have had, had my father managed to get me to Brussels. I probably would have emigrated to the US as did my cousins, Phillip Tauber, Inge

Grosser and George Grosser, who had managed to get to Brussels in 1938.

While I took the gymnastics course through ORT, Mother took a course making artificial flowers. Did she still believe that Rudi Guth would help her to get out of occupied Europe or had she tied her fate to his, regardless of the consequences? My gymnastic course was given in a loft in the Dlouha Trida, one of the main streets leading to the Jewish Quarters of Prague from the center. The teachers for that course were Fredy Hirsch, Jenda Mautner, and a woman by the name of Miriam. I've forgotten her last name. The course was excellent and we studied not merely the practice of gymnastics, but also anatomy and physiology. The most important connection I made in that course that helped determine my future was that I became good friends with Fredy Hirsch. Thanks partly to Fredy's intervention I am alive today. Fredy was a professional gymnast who also was a youth leader in the Jewish Community of Prague.

After finishing the gymnastics course, I took a cosmetology course. I don't know if I would have ever known how to work for a real life cosmetics firm, or beautician, but it made me feel I was doing something to combat the hopelessness of the situation of being at the mercy of the Nazis. At that time I had to work for the so-called labor assignment corps (*Arbeitseinsatz.*). I worked in a warehouse in the Klimentska, a street in the first borough, where the Nazis collected all the furniture and household goods stolen from Jewish apartments. The party members would come there and choose the most beautiful sets of china, and rugs and glass for practically nothing, and I had to pack their choices for delivery. I was paid very little but at least it was something. That warehouse was part of the expropriation organization of the Nazis. At that time (1941), the first transports of Jews had started to be deported, and the furniture and property collected in the warehouse came of course from the confiscated properties of the deportees.

In the summer of 1941 an ordinance was issued that all Jews had to move into the borough of Vinohrady, and that each family would be allotted one room. We were assigned to a flat in the Perunove 4, a side street off one of the main streets, Vinohradska. That was the neighborhood where the Jewish recreational facilities, the Maccabi sports stadium, as well as the Jewish cemetery, were located.

In October the transports from Prague to Litzmannsstadt (formerly Lodz), began. It was not totally unexpected, because rumors had been flying about possible deportations. But no one knew where the transports were to be sent. Fredy Hirsch immediately organized a group of his former gymnastics course students and many Jewish youngsters from the Maccabi Stadium into the so-called "transport assistance" unit (*Transporthilfe*). We would collect the luggage of people who had been assigned to be taken on the transport on the night preceding their removal and bring it to the Veletrzni Palace, the fairgrounds building that had been

64

designated as "*Umschlagplatz*," the point of departure for Jews. In the morning the victims were to assemble at the Veletrzni Palace and from there were marched in groups through the streets of Prague to the freight station from where the trains left for Litzmanstadt. Since these marches occurred around eight or nine in the morning the whole town saw the columns march to the freight station. No one alive at that time can say today that he did not know what was going on. People stood and stared silently, some grinned, some cried, some looked disturbed, but they all saw.

The *Transporthilfe* units would meet the night before at the Jewish community office building in the Pariska, the main street of the Jewish Quarter, and each group received a list of addresses and the name of the moving van which we would use to collect the luggage. The first few transports in late 1941 consisted of Jewish immigrants from Germany and Austria. Of course there were many elderly people among them who could not possibly carry the fifty kgs. of luggage allowed them. We would start on our round about 10-11 in the evening. The moving vans were horse-drawn and I will never forget the sound of these heavy hoofs clip-clopping through the deserted streets of the city.

Rumors came back from Litzmansstadt about the horrible living conditions in the Ghetto: death, disease, and starvation were the daily occurrences. At that time, however, hope for salvation from such a fate came from a member of the Jewish community itself: the suggestion for a Ghetto in the Czech area where there would be the possibility for Jews to survive the War and be spared the deportations to Poland. Jacob Edelstein,[2] the head of the immigration department of the Jewish Community--and by that time immigration was no longer possible--had suggested to the Nazis just such a Ghetto

---

[2] Jacob Edelstein (1903-1944) was the first *Judenältester*, head of the *Judenrat*, Council of Elders, the nominal governing body in Theresienstadt, from 1941-43. He was accused of falsifying documents and shot by the Nazis in 1944.

for the Czech Jews who would work for the German war effort.

Unfortunately, Edelstein did not know the depth of Nazi duplicity. They supported him wholeheartedly for his great idea, but failed to tell him that just such a Ghetto, devised for the purpose of deceiving the free world into believing the Jews were well treated, was being considered before Edelstein even thought of it. Since the rumors of the ghettoes and killings in Poland seemed to have reached the outside world, the Nazis wanted to prevent any more details about the real conditions of the Jews being revealed. Who knows what motivated them: fear of discovery of their real intentions, or their insane pride in their pretended humanity which might be tarnished with such rumors. Nevertheless, they established Theresienstadt.[3] The deception of Edelstein was complete.

---

[3] In <u>Prague in the Shadow of the Swastika</u> .London: Quartet Books, 1995, Colin McDonald and Jan Kaplan describe in detail the Nazi intentions for the town. "50-60,000 are to be concentrated in Terezin (Theresienstadt). From there the Jews will be taken East. Utmost secrecy

67

The first transports to Theresienstadt occurred beginning in January 1942, after the camp was established in November 1941. The first two were called A-KI and A-KII *Aufbaukommando* (construction work detail) and consisted of laborers and specialists to prepare Theresienstadt to become the "Prima Ghetto," the deceptive title that was meant for the deportees as well as for the free world.[4]

Before I and my mother were deported, I had acquired another boyfriend, Jirka Wachtel. He was a very kind and loving young man; not as artistic and talented as Pips, but he loved me and was very good to me. His family was quite wealthy, but, of course, also in reduced circumstances as we all were. They had had a villa in the best neighborhood of Prague, but lived now in one room like every other Jewish family in the city. They did, however, have more resources than Mother and I, being natives of

---

was planned. The Jews were to think it was a labor camp, not a transit camp "(p.121).

[4] Ruth Bondy, Elder of the Jews : Jakob Edelstein of Theresienstadt. New York: Grove Press, 1981.

Prague with better connections. Jirka would sometimes bring me tidbits, such as sausage, or chocolate or cheese: things that the average person could not buy with food stamps and food stamps were our only means for buying groceries. You had to know where the delicacies, or items not obtainable with the food stamps were available, and Mother and I did not have such connections. I was extremely grateful for Jirka's help, and I needed him very much, someone to love me. My self-confidence was practically non-existent. After Pips had left at the beginning of 1941 I had no boyfriend, and having a boyfriend was important at that point. Not only could it give me protection on the street, but, having incredibly little money, it meant that some of the necessities like extra food were provided by a man.

In the Perunova we lived with two other families in a three-room apartment with kitchen and bath and a small foyer in the middle. The actual tenants of the flat was the Benda family: a married couple and one small girl. They, of course, occupied the largest room. The second room was occupied by a young couple whose name I forgot. The only thing I remember about them is that the husband took an ice cold shower every morning. The room assigned to Mother and me was long and narrow. I presume it was originally meant to be the maid's room. There was just enough room for two beds along the walls and one wardrobe. The kitchen was accessible in rotation, just as the bathroom was. Any time for intimacy for me and Jirka could only be had when Mother would spend the night with her lover.

In April of 1942, Mother and I received the dreaded notice for transport. I am always asked by my students and listeners in my lectures, "Where and how were you arrested?" And I have to explain to them that Jews were not arrested. As in so many other situations, the Nazis showed their incredible cynicism. They tricked the Jews into becoming their co-perpetrators by forcing the Jewish communities in the various occupied countries to organize the arrangements for the calling up of the victims, for preparing the so-called *Umschlagplatz* for the deportation as I've already mentioned. The *Umschlagplatz* in Prague was the fairgrounds on the Letna, the Veletrzni Palace. And thus it was that Mother and I received a very polite card, informing us that we were going on transport on May 7; that we could take 50 kg of luggage, a bedroll and food for two days, and that we had to leave all our other property in place.

One strange thing sticks in my mind of these last days. I had had a mild flirtation the previous year with a well-known tennis star named Jirka Krasny. Shortly before the transport date, there arrived a bouquet of white roses for me addressed to Duschitchka. "Duschitchka" had been his pet name for me.

Chapter Four

Theresienstadt: May 1942-January 1943

I seem to have a block about my memories of Theresienstadt, and I don't know why. It certainly was not half as bad a time as Birkenau; on the contrary. When asked about Theresienstadt, I always say: "I wish I could have spent the War in Theresienstadt instead of Birkenau." I know there are plenty of books on the order of Arnost Lustig's or, among others, Carlo Rossi's, who described Theresienstadt as "Hell's vestibule."[1] I wonder whether either ever was deported to Birkenau and had a moment to realize that Theresienstadt had given him a chance to live that he did not appreciate. There

---

[1] Arnost Lustig (1926--) a Czech writer who was a Holocaust survivor, has written, among other works on his experience, Night and Hope, a collection of stories (1962) which was made into the Czech film "Return from Paradise" (1963), and the novel Diamonds of the Night (1987). Lustig was deported to Auschwitz where his father died.

were plenty of deprivations in Theresienstadt: hunger, and dirt, and disease. But, unless you went "on transport" to Auschwitz, you could die your own death. Was it guilt that makes me block out my memories of the camp that I did not join my Mother in going immediately "East" which turned out to be a death sentence? Or was it that I somehow have repressed this chapter in my Hegira to hell, since I was not particularly proud of my behavior there.

Be that as it may, I am not going to delve into the psychological reasons for my reluctance; we lived life as much as we could there, and we young ones grabbed as much of every life-confirming act as we dared. Was it morally defensible? Probably in the eyes of my Mother it would not have been, and thinking back as a mother myself, I would not approve of such behavior. But then my actions were totally defensible and normal and logical; only my still functioning restricted upbringing reveals itself when I write these lines. Under normal circumstances I would be ashamed of such uninhibited "sleeping around," but then nothing was "normal."[2] Wives slept with other women's husbands and vice versa, and being there by myself, my innate need to be needed and loved by someone again manifested itself in my mistaking sexual activity for fulfillment of that need.

I could probably skip the 8 months in Theresienstadt without reducing significantly the impact of my story, but this period was part of my growing up in the sense that it was the first time that I was absolutely alone, and not accountable to anyone. Perhaps that fact contributed to my lack of inhibitions.

When on May 9, 1942, we arrived in Theresienstadt (a garrison town, built in 1780 by

---

[2] "The reaction of the younger people to the atmosphere of doom pervading the Ghetto found its expression in the ardent desire to enjoy what pleasures they could find . . . only the present was real and the best way to fight its depressing effects was by the pursuit of pleasure, in particular sexual pleasure." Zdenek Lederer, Ghetto Theresienstadt. London: Edward Gladstone and Son, 1953. p. 123. See also Norbert Troller, Theresienstadt, Hitler's 'Gift' to the Jews. Translated by Susan Czernyak-Spatz, edited by Joel Shatzky. Chapel Hill: University of North Carolina Press, 1991; 2004.

Emperor Josef of Austria, son of Maria Theresa, and named after his mother), Mother and I were sent to the Hohenelbe barracks, part of the hospital compound for the so-called quarantine.[3] One of the major benefits to the Reich of the persecution of the Jews was the biggest official robbery campaign in modern history which had been going on since 1933. Therefore the Nazis must have figured that the transport victims from Prague had already been fleeced in their domiciles and there was not much of value left to be had from the 50-kg. luggage packs of the victims.

I am sure that after all this time those of us who were not sent "East" from an arriving transport realize by now that what occurred in the Hohenelbe quarantine that May morning in

---

[3] In most documentary films about Theresienstadt the Jaeger barracks is designated as the area for quarantine. However, Lederer confirms that during the first year, 1942, until the arrival of the Austrian and German transports during the summer of 1942, the Czech transports were quarantined in the Hohenelbe. He also confirmed my assertion that the searches at the time of my arrival, May, 1942, were not as rigorous as later (p.38). I distinctly remember having my luggage almost intact under my sleeping bag and pillow in the Hamburger barracks.

1942, and during any subsequent transport arriving from wherever into Theresienstadt, was a "selection." That was the process that became famous or rather infamous at the Birkenau ramp: The SS men pointing their finger to left or right: life or death in the gas chamber. Perhaps the SS was not standing there and pointing "right" and "left." It was only the administrative and professional hierarchy of Theresienstadt that came to examine every new transport, and "selected" who was to stay and who was to go on to the "East." At the time no one knew what "the East" meant. But those who did go "East" were never heard from again.

After the War, it became evident to the rest of the world what the word meant: Sobibor, Maidanek, Chelmno, Treblinka and Belzec:[4]

---

[4] There were three basic categories of camps in the Nazi system. In Auschwitz, Auschwitz I was a concentration camp; Auschwitz II-Birkenau, was a death camp; Auschwitz III-Buna or Monowitz, was a labor camp for I.G. Farben. The ultimate purpose of all three, of course, was to promote the "Final Solution." Sobibor and Maidanek were located near Lublin, Poland and Chelmno in Western Poland. Treblinka was on the Bug River in the Western Ukraine and Belzec was in Poland.

places of no return, extermination camps. Nothing was said about those destinations in Theresienstadt at that time. Among the administrators "selecting" at the Hohenelbe was Fredy Hirsch. Having been designated as a member of the "*Judenrat*" by the Nazis, he was the assigned youth welfare administrator. When he saw me and my mother, he immediately said to us: "You and your mother are staying here."

Mother, of course, asked whether her lover, Rudi Guth, could also stay. Fredy said he regretted that that was impossible since Rudi was not part of the family, whereupon Mother said: "Then we don't stay either." To this day I don't know where I suddenly found the courage to defy my mother for the first time in my life. I said "No, I am staying; if you want to you can stay with me, but I am staying." Mother was absolutely beside herself. She must have had a premonition that we would never meet again, and I will never know if perhaps things flashed through her mind of where she had landed herself and me due to her refusal to join my father. Her love for Rudi was stronger than her love and concern for me.

"We shall meet for Christmas at the Prasna Brana," I said. These were the last words I remember saying to my mother. At that time the Battle of Stalingrad had ended as a disastrous defeat for the German army which lost almost 150,000 soldiers, and there was hope in the air that the war would end soon. Well, my war for survival had just started. But I remember Mother shaking her head out of the train window. Did she know?

Almost 50 years later I took my three children to Auschwitz and Birkenau. In the Auschwitz Museum I found the transport lists of the train that contained my mother's name. It had ended in the gas chambers of Sobibor. These transport lists were the only records of the thousands who, without a trace, went into the gas chambers of the first five extermination camps already mentioned.

Those of us who had been selected to stay were taken to the Hamburger barracks, the women, that is. All of us found a space on the floor for our bedroll with all our possessions in the suitcase at the head. I suppose at that point there was not as much stealing occurring as it did later. Of course, there was no way to lock anything up. The barracks had military- type washrooms and lavatories, which, according to Norbert Troller's diary, <u>Theresienstadt: Hitler's "Gift" to the Jews</u> (See f. 2), were a lot more than what the civilian houses in Theresienstadt had when the Jews arrived there. That Theresienstadt is today a town with modern sanitation or at least cesspool installations and running water was only thanks to the work of the Jews in this ante -chamber to destruction.

The room I was assigned to was directly opposite the food-distribution counter in the Hamburger barracks. The Hamburger was built like all the other barracks, with the exception of the Sudeten, the Kavalier barracks, and the Jäger barracks. These three corresponded to the star-shape protrusions of the bulwark. Theresienstadt, built in the late eighteenth century, was designed in the then common architectural star shape for fortified garrisons. Some of the barracks were built into the star-shaped protrusions of the wall, such as the above mentioned "*Kasernen*" (barracks). The rest of the barracks were four-square buildings with either one or two courtyards in the middle, probably used for drilling exercises for the military, and arcades around the two floors from which the rooms opened up. That arrangement had the great advantage that at least the rooms had cross ventilation if the doors stayed open, which they did in the summer of 1942; because with at least 20 women to a room, we needed ventilation badly. As long as I was there the two big windows stayed open most of the time. That was, of course, before there were bunks. All of our meager possessions that we had been able to keep through our ordeals were placed at the head of the "bed." Strangely enough nothing was locked, nothing was watched. From what I learned after the War from reports of Thersienstadt in 1943 and 1944, such relatively ideal conditions did not prevail for long after I left.

I remember having kept my belongings intact because I had a green and dark-red plaid blanket in my luggage and it had become the fashion to make bias cut-skirts out of the blankets. Women did not stop wanting some kind of new clothes, just because it seemed impossible to get them. Most every woman had the plaid blankets, and of course there were enough women there at that time who had been seamstresses in private life. I don't remember what I paid for having the skirt made, but it had, of course, to be paid with foodstuff. I probably got some bread from my baker friends in the Kavalier barracks #2, the one that housed the bakery.

I found many of my friends from Prague in the camp. Theresienstadt was a great leveler of social differences. That is how I became friends with Lilly Pohnert. Lilly had been in an exclusive circle in Prague to which I had no access. She belonged to the wealthy, native Prague Jews.

Lilly had been deported to Theresienstadt with her new husband, Honza Pohnert. I don't remember what her maiden name was. I only remember that Lilly was not too keen on her husband, who was a bit of a *schlump,* rather dull. Lilly was very vivacious, short and blonde. Even in Theresienstadt she was very well dressed. I seem to remember that Lilly was in the room with me in the Hamburger.

Her sister in-law, Honza's sister, visited her there. I don't remember where she lived, but her husband was from the AK-I, the pioneer transport, mentioned above, and therefore one of the aristocrats of the camp. So it can be assumed that they had their own *kumbal,* a private room that was often built in the large vaults or in the stairwells of the fortress.[5] For the life of me, I don't remember his name. I only remember he was dark-haired, stocky and well-built. He was my first fling, in the corner of one of

---

[5] In his memoir of Theresienstadt, Norbert Troller records how he specifically designed these kumbals in exchange for food and special privileges. See Theresienstadt: Hitler's 'Gift' to the Jews, pp.110-116.

the colonnades. As I said, that was my way of building some self-esteem. I really was lucky that I neither got pregnant, nor contracted any diseases. Thinking back, that should have been one of my big concerns, but it wasn't.

Lilly worked in the nursery when we first met. In spite of what so many survivors of the youth homes in Theresienstadt proclaim to have suffered, it was the administration's most urgent task and greatest concern to provide for the infants, children and adolescents in Theresienstadt. There were separate children's homes, starting with the infant nurseries, for small children, for school-age children and for teen-agers.

The Jewish administration's greatest concerns were these homes. Working for the Youth Welfare Department, thanks to Fredy Hirsch, it was my job to scrounge school materials for the children's homes, such as pencils, paper, and other supplies. The children were given the next largest rations, right after the laborers. Only then came the rest of the population and, last and the least to be considered, the old people.[6]

Though Lilly never in her life had been nearer to nursing than to have a hospital nurse wait on her, she had, with her charm, wangled the very desirable position of nurse in the infant house.

Sometimes in the evenings Lilly and I and some other single girls like us would walk across the little park behind the Hamburger barracks (after June 1942, when the town became open for Jews to move around freely) to the bakery in the back of the Kavalier barrack # 2.

I don't remember his name, but one of the bakers, a red-headed Czech-speaking young man, would always give us some bread, which, of course, considering the small rations, was a Godsend. I had brought with me an old-fashioned pocket knife, the kind with a

---

[6] A children's kitchen was opened. There the children had more and better-prepared food than the adults. Stray parcels provided the children with additional nutrition. Lederer, p.133.

corkscrew and another small blade. It might sound strange that I had a quite sharp pocket knife in my possession after the search of my luggage. However at that time, short of a revolver or an actual dagger, I don't think anyone thought in terms of security to confiscate every nail file or manicure scissors. All the Nazis were concerned about when they were rifling through the luggage were items they could use for themselves or turn into money. I used the knife to slice bread one day and holding the bread in my left hand and cutting with my trusty knife vigorously, stabbed it into the ball of my thumb. I don't think there was a first-aid clinic as there were later in all the barracks. It was probably one of the *Stubenälteste* (dorm supervisors) who put a bandage on the cut. I doubt whether she put any disinfectant beyond iodine tincture on it. Anyway, it did heal, without infection, and to this day I can look at the ball of my left thumb and see my "Theresienstadt scar."

It seems to me that right from the beginning of my time in Theresienstadt there were clandestine performances of cabarets and music in some places. I myself preferred the jazz music performances. Though Gideon Klein was a good friend of mine from Prague, I somehow did not crave classical music. I preferred the jazz we used to adore, like Django Reinhardt's, a well-known French jazz guitarist of the 1930's, and Benny Goodman's or of the Dorsey Brothers. Jirka Goldschmidt and Jirka Taussig were probably the forerunners of the Ghetto Swingers, a jazz group established in Theresienstadt that, among other daring antics, performed a "Bugle Call Rag" on the occasion of the visit of the Red Cross to Theresienstadt in 1944. Since Jirka Taussig was the permanent boyfriend of Gaby Meisl, it was Gaby who got to sing with the group, though I wanted that job badly. From the end of 1942 on, the *Freizeitgestaltungs* (leisure time) Department set up not only cabarets and concert performances of operas, but also produced one of the most famous children's operas of the 20th century, Hans Krasa's "Brundibar" which is making the rounds of the theaters of the world to this day and was made into a children's book by Maurice Sendak. So, of course, we, the young ones, tried to take advantage of every form of entertainment we could find.

I ran into Harry Tressler at one of those entertainments, a reception of some bigwig in the Administration.[7] I did not realize until after the war that Harry had been an integral part of the administration, being practically Edelstein's adjutant. To me he was a nice-looking guy who seemed to have connections, which was always important in Theresienstadt, and who seemed to like me. But the affair ended on a sour note. Harry tried to make love to me in his private *kumbal,* in which he, of course, as a member of the administration was quartered. He failed

---

[7] A group of Jewish community leaders had been recruited from the Jewish Community in Prague, most of them ardent Zionists, who tried to run the camp somewhat on the model of a Kibbutz. They tried to divide what little food there was according to what every inmate's position was in the camp. One of the saddest results of this effort was the near starvation of the elderly since they did not count in the workforce and therefore received the smallest rations. See Troller, pp.53, & 93.

miserably and I still can see his disgusted face, whether he hated himself, or me for not having aroused him enough. Whatever it was I never saw Harry again in Theresienstadt.

It must have been around that time that Lilly was transferred from the nursery to the boys' home as an in-house nurse. The boys' home was right next to the wooden fence that separated the SS quarters from the town. I remember the fence closing off the street right next to the boys' house. Behind it we could see a park.

Lilly was determined that we would get out of the Hamburger barracks and have our own *kumbal,* as any private space was called. ("*Kumbal"* is the Czech word for small chamber). Lilly had found such a space opposite the boys' home, a stable in the yard of a private house. It was a small stable at that, but it had a door and a window. I seem to remember that it had electricity, because I know we did not use candles or a kerosene lamp. I don't remember how long it took us to clean out the accumulated dirt of many years; I remember we got two wooden bed-frames and two mattresses on which we put our sleeping bags and blankets. The mattresses and frames must have been "*geschleust*"[8] because we had actually no right to that *kumbal* and could not have requested beds or anything for the *kumbal* from the Ghetto administration. Lilly, ever artistic, painted small wooden boards with the titles of our favorite songs, and decorations, which we affixed over our beds. Mine was Lehar's *"Schatz ich bitt' Dich komm heut' Nacht."* ("Darling, I beg you, love me tonight.")

That was the favorite song of Dr. Ernstl Fuchs and me. It must have been in late summer of 1942 when I had met him. I don't know whether he was already a doctor or just a medical student, but he worked in the hospital ward in one of the barracks; I think it was the

---

[8] Illegally obtained, as were the more valuable possessions of the inmates as they were "sluiced" through "inspection" when they first arrived with their belongings. The word had taken on the connotation of "illegally obtaining" anything in Theresienstadt.

Sudeten. When we became acquainted, he had a girlfriend, a very pretty blonde nurse, who worked in the Hohenelbe. She, however, fell ill with typhus. Ernstl kept visiting her dutifully, but in the meantime, as it happened, we had fallen in love.

It was a wonderful time for me despite the fact that we were incarcerated in a camp run by the Nazis. Being in love was important in Theresienstadt, though the object of one's affection might change. It was not only important to have someone who could help with providing some extra food, which Ernstl could do, working in the hospital in the Sudeten barracks. It was also part of your social standing to be permanently attached to someone who was available. Most married men were available for one-night stands, or rather one stolen hour in some corner of the fortress. An almost permanent relationship was a rarity.

We would walk on the ramparts, share what food we had cooked on the little potbellied stove that a friend had "*schleussed*" for us. That stove was Lilly's and my undoing. It turned out the stove was stolen from the lumber yard, and a Ghetto policeman pressed the boy who had stolen it to tell them whom he had given it to. That is how we both got into the transport to Birkenau. Lilly went first. I had Ernstl give me a shot of typhoid serum, which caused fever, which I hoped would prevent my deportation, but my illness did not last long. I remember I begged some friends in the Sudeten barracks, the men's barracks, to hide me. I don't remember who they were. I just remember my desperation.

Saying goodbye to Ernstl was the worst feeling I had ever experienced until then. I, of course, did not anticipate what awaited us at the end of the journey, and therefore was more heartbroken about the separation from what I thought was my great love, or was he? I saw Ernstl once more, in September of 1943, when I was already in the *Schreibstube* (Central Administration) in Birkenau, in Block 4 of the B1b camp. The Sauna of B1b, located next to our block, was used for processing in new transports, men and women, and he was among a group of newly processed-in men from Theresienstadt. That was the last time I ever saw him. Who knows if he survived?[9]

Anyway, nothing helped me out of my situation of "going on transport." It was my good fortune, however, and that of all the people on that transport, that a fairly large group of deportees from the west must have come in a day or so ahead of our scheduled departure. Those were the people that were told they were going to a Spa for the duration of the War. They were people especially selected by the Nazis to serve as quasi hostages in case they might lose the War. So-called *"Prominente,"* they were usually well-known personages from the countries of origin, or in case of some German Jews, they were prominent veterans of World War I whom Hitler had promised would be safe

---

[9] According to an online report of the Stockholm International Conference on the Holocaust, January 26-28, 2000, of the 57,628 men, women and children who were deported from Theresienstadt, only 6008 returned.

from deportation. Of course, they could not be deported in cattle cars which would make their fate too obvious. So they were brought to Theresienstadt in old-fashioned pre-World War I passenger cars.[10]. And of course if one of those passenger car trains stood on the siding in Bauschowitz, why get cattle cars for the transport ready for the East? So, lucky for us, we were shipped "East" in the passenger cars.

There were toilets at each end of the cars; dirty, stinking, but toilets. And benches to sit on. It was luxurious compared to the cattle cars that so many of the other victims went on which often resulted in exhaustion that could lead to death. We could see we were going east from the rising and setting sun. But we were certainly not prepared for what awaited us on Jan. 31, 1943, or perhaps it was Feb. 1, for that is the record they have of my arrival date in the

---

[10] Theresienstadt, the Germans had intimated, was a sort of resort. Before their departure the "resettlers" were told to take with them all their possessions--confiscated at their arrival--and some of them were even induced to purchase deeds of lease entitling them to a special place in the Ghetto for the Aged. Lederer, p.39.

archives at Beit Terezin, a kibbutz founded in Israel by survivors of Theresienstadt. Whatever date it was, however it was recorded in the book of history, for me it was the time of my arrival in hell.

Chapter Five
Auschwitz-Birkenau: the First Day
January 31, 1943

Whatever preceded this narrative was the first chapter in my life. The second one, the creation of a new person, the trial by fire literally, started now.

When in the course of my numerous lectures that I give to high school or college students about my experiences during the Holocaust, I make the assertion that I considered myself lucky to have been sent ONLY to Birkenau, and not to have passed through one of the Polish Ghettos, I get uncomprehending stares, until I explain that in my view, the Ghettoes were the most horrifying locations of human cruelty, perpetrated by young men, mostly, who had been given a free hand, by fiat of their superiors, to indulge in the lowest instincts humanity has known, probably since the middle ages if not even earlier at a time in which there were no limits to the level of human cruelty. [1]

This is what I was spared when I found myself on the train with the destination "Auschwitz." We had left Theresienstadt and Bauschowitz behind and proceeded in an easterly direction, judging by the sun, which we could see, because we were in an old-fashioned passenger railway car. The rail line built between Bauschowitz and Theresienstadt was not finished until October 1943. After that time the transports were shipped directly from the Jägerkaserne in Theresienstadt proper, where the rail line to Auschwitz ended. The

---

[1] "There are more than enough glimpses of what might be called the sporting beast-for example an SS officer's playful execution of a young Jewish mother with a baby on her shoulder, to whom the officer had, a moment before, given a loaf of bread. Or this recorded by a woman: 'One day a small boy was killed on Biala Street as he attempted to pull a carrot lying in the gutter on the Aryan side through a hole in the fence. A German spotted him, inserted his gun in the hole and killed the boy...' Through such scenes runs a vibration of Caligula's boast: 'Remember: I can do anything to anyone': the pleasure that power takes in its own vicious freedom." Lance Morrow, *Time*, October 28, 2002, p.69. Review of <u>Words to Outlive Us: Eyewitness Accounts from the Warsaw Ghetto</u>, Michael Grynberg, ed. New York: Metropolitan Books, 2002.

"*Prominente*" passenger train on which we were traveling, and which had arrived the night before our departure, was probably a life saver for many of us on our journey. Cattle cars, the usual mode of Jewish transports, caused the death of many people by asphyxiation, or dehydration. We did not move very fast, I presume because of military trains on the line ahead of us.

The Russian front was already crumbling, therefore the rail lines were badly clogged. We spent at least one night on the train, maybe two. We had wooden benches to sit on, albeit the cars were a bit crowded. It must have been bitter cold that January 31 or February 1, 1943 when we arrived in Auschwitz. Strangely, I did not remember the cold, though I am sure the train was not heated. There must have been enough body heat to keep us fairly warm. Besides that we wore all the warm clothing we could manage to pile on us.

Sometime during what must have been the second night on the train, it stopped at a brightly lit platform. We must have passed through the now-infamous towered archway leading into the Birkenau compound. No one noticed it. The train stopped, the doors were flung open, and the very first impression was a smell, or, more accurately, a repulsive stink, seemingly emanating from a smokestack in the background of the train, its flames topped by black swirling clouds.

Though my friend who also survived the camp, Zippi Tichauer, (née Spitzer), who came in 1942 with one of the Slovakian transports, swears up and down that in January of 1943 no crematorium was built yet, I am convinced that a large smokestack was smoking in the background facing the locomotive. Even Danuta Czech[2] talks of Cremo 2 and 3 as having been finished in the first half of 1943. According to a letter from the Central Construction department, dated January 29, 1943, a crematorium was

---

[2] Kalendarium der Ereignisse im Konzentrationslager Auschwitz-Birkenau, 1939-1945. Reinbek bei Hamburg:Rowohlt Verlag 1989.

finished and test fired.[3] Could they have done a test firing at the time of our arrival? They must have been burning prisoners somewhere[4] and the smoke and the flames were clearly visible to us at the time of our arrival. It is quite possible that what we saw were the flames from the bunkers I and II, called *"Das weisse Haus"* (the white house), and *"Das rote Haus"* (the red house) that were used in Birkenau as temporary crematoriums, and the flames and smoke might have been from the pyres where the bodies were burned.[5] A footnote in Czech's book describes the bunkers as having been disguised as farm buildings so as to look innocuous to the approaching victims. Rooms inside had been prepared for use as gas chambers.

The ubiquitous *"Raus, raus"* ("Get out, get out!") sounded and we hurried to comply though at that time we had not seen the whips and

---

[3] Czech, p. 397.

[4] Czech states at one point during the date of our arrival, January 31, 1943: " 2341 prisoners, among them 750 children sent to the gas chamber," p. 400.

[5] Czech, pp. 187, 209, 211 and 277.

dogs, which supposedly greeted every transport in Birkenau. We found ourselves standing on what appeared to be a fairly wide railroad platform, bordered on both sides by long barbed wire fences. We could see neither the beginning nor the end of the fences; they were braced by concrete poles that bent inward away from the platform. There were wooden observation towers spaced at regular intervals along the fences.

The fences as well as the towers had very bright lights on them. After the War, the only analogy I could use to describe the first impression of those lights greeting us was the sight of a petroleum refinery with its lights strung at regular intervals just like the camps at night. Only I, living in an America innocent of such memories, could see a sinister connotation in that harmless sight.

I am trying to recreate the situation at the platform. Facing us, where we had gotten off the train, stood a field- gray ambulance. It had the Red Cross logo on the side and on the hood, a veritable sign of security for any civilized person in the twentieth century, to whom this red cross represented safety and international goodwill.

This ambulance never carried a sick or injured person during its entire existence. It was the perfect psychological foil to keep the arriving people from realizing that the last thing they would find here was security. The Nazis may have despised Freud, but Lord did they know how to avail themselves of every psychological deception that might have had its origin in Sigmund Freud's teachings! Especially feigning security where there was none. The false pretenses started with Theresienstadt and ended for millions at the entrance to the gas chambers, disguised to look like substantial farmhouses.[6] The pragmatic purpose for the ambulances was to carry the tins of Cyclon B gas to the crematorium and bring the empty tins back.

---

[6] According to testimony given by the Nazi Dr. Eduard Wirths in a war crimes trial after the war. Herman Langbein. Menschen in Auschwitz. Frankfurt: Ullstein Buch #33014, 1972.

It might seem strange but I only remember that we women were lining up in rows of five next to the train. I do not remember where the men lined up. From what I learned later it must have been on the other side of the train. There were men in field-gray SS-uniforms and men in what seemed gray and blue-striped pants and jackets. The men in gray and blue wore brimless round caps. I believe they were striped as well, and these men seemed to all be bald. They looked neither dirty nor emaciated. What we did not know, of course, was that these men were from the "*Kanada*" commando,[7] the work detail in charge of the prisoners' possessions, the elite detail of the Birkenau camp.

An SS man in a very well-tailored uniform with officer's insignias as well as a medical insignia positioned himself in front of the column of women. Next to him stood a non-commissioned SS-man in a less well-tailored

---

[7] "Commando" would be the German equivalent of "unit" or, in military parlance, "detail."

uniform. They surveyed the first row of women, standing in front of them. Some women in the row were sent to the tarp-covered trucks lined up on the ramp in front of the ambulance. The rest were told they would walk. I was standing well back in the column and could observe that a certain pattern seemed to evolve. Girls under 14 or 15, or if they looked under that age, and women over 35-40, would go by truck. All children with their mothers in the column went into the truck as well. I remember thinking: "How lucky they are to be able to ride. Now we remnants will have to walk God knows how far." At that point those of us left standing did not realize what we learned all too soon: that the trucks took the women and children chosen "to ride" directly to the gas chamber and the crematorium.

We remnants--there were only 62 of us that remained out of approximately 500 women in our half of the transport of a thousand "pieces," which was the usual designation of Jews sent on transport-- were walked through a gate in the fence facing the ramp on the left side in front of the crematorium and were herded into a pre-fab barrack with a dirt floor and a few dim lights: nothing more. Prisoner-guards were waiting for us in the barrack, women of our age in civilian clothing with broad red stripes down the back and kerchiefs tied tightly behind their heads to cover what seemed to be their shaved skulls. A number was sown on the left side of their clothing in the vicinity of the heart.

After we had been told to sit on the dirt floor, huddled in the bitter January cold, they walked among us and asked us to give them any jewelry or valuables we had on us. The SS would take them anyway, so why would we not give it to Jewish girls who could help themselves with it? We did not know that these girls were young Slovak and Polish Jews who had already survived several months in camp, and who by dint of their survival had each managed to garner a "position'" inside the camp. The first Slovakian transports had arrived in Auschwitz, the main camp, between March and May of

1942. They were housed there in 10 blocks that had been separated by barbed wire from the rest of the camp. I remember giving away a locket that Ernstl had presented to me. It had nothing in it, but it was a very pretty baroque-style locket. Somehow I realized that it was better the girls should have it.

The prisoner night guards, as they were called in the quarantine barrack, had all been in camp already from March, May or June, 1942.[8] The night guards were all too eager to answer our questions about where we were and what had happened to those who had gone in the trucks. They told us every incredible fact about Birkenau, including the sight and smell we had noted when leaving the train. Thinking back, I sometimes have the feeling as if these girls were delighted to tell us what was awaiting us, and what had happened to the families of the women

---

[8] It isn't widely known that the Slovaks under "Father" Jozef Tiso--an ordained priest and collaborator with the Nazis who was appointed by them as "President" of Slovakia as that part of what was the former Czech Republic was called--paid the Germans to deport the Jews.

in the barrack. Perhaps there was a certain amount of envy because we all still looked quite civilized--most of us had the then fashionable long hairdos--and due to having ridden in the passenger train, we were not as disheveled and filthy as transports that had arrived in freight cars. The descriptions of the gas chamber and the crematorium were quite detailed, probably enriched by these guards' fantasy and by rumors. They did not really have the precise descriptions, but what they told was met with incredulous stares.

Who in the 20th century, even living under the Hitler regime in Ghettoes, under cruel chicanery, could imagine such inhumanity? Such things did not happen in reality. But they did. We refused to believe the facts when they were given us right there. Any wonder that the free world, only hearing of such inhumane atrocities, would reject them as unbelievable. Having come on the transport by myself, I remained very calm in the face of all the unbelievable information we were given by the prisoner-guards. Sometimes I wonder whether that was a symptom of the kind of shock that I had experienced, because I remember later, during the processing-in, I also remained strangely detached. We stayed the whole night in the "quarantine barrack." It was interesting how the Nazis used scientific words, like "quarantine," which has the meaning of keeping diseased animals or people from contaminating others, to designate the most inhuman processes such as making people wait overnight on the dirt floor, without food or water, to be stripped of their individuality and their humanity.

I suppose they processed a previously arrived transport in the Sauna during the night because, as far as I know, the Sauna was never unoccupied night or day during that winter and early spring. In the morning we were led to be processed-in. This took place in the Sauna, a real Sauna, with heating and showers, which served mainly as the processing center for the transports. Only rarely was it used for its original purpose.

We were put into a large room with recessed windows. Young SS-men were sitting in these recesses as guards. We were told to strip completely. Again I can only say, I must have been in shock, feeling as if I was standing outside of myself observing the proceedings. I calmly took off all my clothes and the felt boots I was wearing. Then we were shorn from top to bottom of all body-hair. I think I remember that it was women who sheared us. This was supposedly for hygienic purposes, but in reality it was just one of the numerous processes calculated to demean and dehumanize the person, so that no dignity, self-esteem, or a sense of the need for self-preservation would be left. I did not have to learn later about the post-war psychological explanations of the dehumanization process. Its aims were very obvious.

Shorn and naked, we were chased into the shower room to be given a one-minute ice-cold shower, nothing provided to dry ourselves. Chased into the next room from the shower room, we found women prisoners behind tables in striped prisoner clothing (they were working in the *"Kleiderkammer,"* a very good work detail) handing out some blue and white striped shifts, and what looked like boxer shorts with strings to tie them. At the next table they handed us khaki-colored pants and long jackets, buttoned to the neck. We learned later that those were the summer uniforms of dead Russian soldiers, bullet holes, blood spatters and all. Probably they were just deloused after the last owner had gone into the gas. I don't know how well this is known but the Russian POW's were not considered POW's but just as much subhuman species as the Jews, to be exterminated with the Slavic people, after the Jews were eliminated. Therefore they were immediately put into an extermination camp, instead of a POW camp, only to be transferred later when the Nazis were ready to exterminate the Slavic people. According to documentation the first Cyclon B experiment in Auschwitz was done on 800 Russian prisoners.

After the pants and jackets came shoes if we were lucky enough to get them. They might not always fit, they might not always match, but they could be usually tied with shoelaces and would stay on the foot. If we were unlucky, we got clogs. Clogs rubbed the foot, caused open sores, resulted in infection, in gangrene, in death. Lucky me; I got shoes, high-tops, if I remember correctly. Of course the shoes, like any other civilian clothing that might be given to the prisoners, were the stuff that was not good enough to be sent into the Reich to be used by the textile-and-clothing-deprived population. I always wondered whether the German population receiving the clothing through the *Winterhilfe*, or other charities, knew that they wore the clothing of dead Jews.

Next came the tattooing on the left forearm. Depending on who did the tattooing, women prisoners trained in doing this, we either got a large sloppy five-digit number or a small neat five-digit number. Either one had a triangle underneath. When the first women prisoners, those of the Slovakian transport, were tattooed, only non-Germans and Jews were so marked but there was no triangle under the Jewish number. Then the SS discovered that identifying a naked Jewish woman was not as easy as identifying a naked Jewish man who stood out from the others by being circumsized, and unless they looked Semitic or of Mediterranean type, women had no identifying mark. And if they were blue eyed to boot, and hairless, there was no way to distinguish them from Aryan women. Therefore, triangles were tattooed under the number of all Jewish women new arrivals, after November or December 1942.[9]

Many of the older Slovakian Jewish women prisoners, who had been tattooed without the triangle, strenuously avoided having the triangle added to their number. Since by that

---

[9] Towards the end of 1942 all women prisoners were tattooed with non-repeated numbers. Numbers from dead prisoners were never reused, in spite of many such claims. There is knowledge of other camps having repeated the numbers by using numbers from dead prisoners. However, this method was never used in the entire Auschwitz complex. Unpublished memoir Zippi Tichauer, July, 1991.

time most Slovakian and Polish Jewish "older numbers," as veterans of the camp were called, already had relatively secure positions, by not having triangle designations they improved their possible chances of survival since only Jewish prisoners could be sent to the gas by selection.

Another part of our uniform was the kerchief which we received to cover our shorn heads. I don't remember what color it was. Whatever it was, it was pretty soon stiff with dirt, because, of course it served for towel and napkin, the only thing that could be used to wipe your face and/or hands. That kerchief had to be tied a certain way, behind the head with the end tucked in at the neck, and woe the prisoner whose kerchief was not tied correctly. During the daily selection, morning and night, a kerchief tied under the chin, because its wearer might be too exhausted to raise her arms to tie it correctly, could mean being sent to the gas.

We were handed a strip of cloth with our number printed on it and a large needle and thread and had to sow the cloth on the left side over the breast on the uniform. Then we were handed the bowl, a brick-red metal bowl about 10 inches wide and about 5 inches deep. This bowl, as we all too soon realized, was the only utensil we were given: no knife, no fork, no spoon, no cup, no saucer, no plate. There were also no toothbrushes, handkerchiefs, towels, nor combs. In a word, we were totally deprived of any civilized accessories; another fiendishly clever aspect of the Nazis' plan to totally dehumanize their victims, which, of course, led to mental dehumanization as a consequence. It reduced the prisoner's self-esteem, her self-awareness, in short her humanity, to zero, preparing her for the quick descent into what in the camp jargon was called the "*Muselmann*" state (zombie) which designated her as ready for the gas. The speed with which a human being, deprived of the simplest necessities, deteriorates into self-neglect, is a frightening sight. The bowl as the sole personal possession of the inmates was the symbol of the lowest level to which the well-thought out calculations of the Holocaust planners reduced their victims.

From the Sauna and the issuance of the rags, the tattooing, the bowl, we were herded into the "quarantine" block. The Nazis had a fondness for the word "quarantine"; what a perfect euphemism for filth and deprivation! That is what they called the new-arrival blocks.

At that time in the camp B1a, which was the women's camp, the quarantine blocks were Blocks 1,2,and 3, the stone blocks which are still standing today and still looking like large chicken houses. The stone blocks had originally been built to house the aforementioned Russian prisoners in camp Birkenau, the extermination camp being constructed since 1942 five kilometers north of the KZ Auschwitz which was a concentration camp, not a death camp, though some mass gassings took place in the Auschwitz I gas chamber. Each barrack was to house 300-400 prisoners on two-tiered bunks, each bunk holding 3-4 prisoners. The floor consisted of hard-stamped dirt. These brick blocks had no washing facilities, no toilets. There was one latrine and one water faucet for each row of three brick buildings.

At any given time, the new arrival blocks, 1, 2, 3, would hold anywhere from 500-800 women. When the Russian compound was changed into the women's camp in August of 1942, pre-fab wooden blocks were added facing the brick blocks across the camp street. Those blocks had three-tiered single bunks and a washroom attached to each pre-fab block. The pre-fab blocks were for the exclusive use of the political non-Jewish prisoners, most of them either German or Polish, with a few French and Czech politicals. The entire Aryan hospital block was also on the Aryan block side in pre-fabs. Jews were housed only in the stone blocks, and if a "new arrival"--and she would be easily spotted because of the filthy Russian uniforms-- were to dare cross the camp street unaccompanied, perhaps looking for water, or some food remnants that might be available from the packages the Aryan prisoners received, and a *Kapo*, or Matron saw her, she risked a good beating.

On January 31, 1943 we new arrivals were led to block 3 in what was then the women's camp.[10] Block 3 was one of the 3 "quarantine" blocks, the Jewish stone blocks. The space in each of the stone blocks, originally designed for 300-400, now housed 500-800 women. This meant we huddled 5-6 in a bunk. All outside work details were housed in the 3 "new arrival" blocks.[11] So, regardless of how many there were, they had to fit into the three blocks, therefore they were crammed most of the time into double the capacity.

The *"stubovas"* were cleaning and maintenance personal consisting of prisoners

---

[10]In June 1943 the women's camp, B1a, was combined with the former men's camp, B1b to form a larger women's camp.

[11] An "outside" work detail, the first work unit that all new arrivals had to join, labored at heavy physical work outside the camp for at least 10 hrs. a day without the use of any tools. This pitiless schedule, combined with the poor nutrition, wore down most of the prisoners, reducing them to "Muselmen" who would then be selected to go to the gas.

who had already survived 8-9 months of Auschwitz and Birkenau, and had been given these very desirable jobs. Those jobs provided extra food, and exemption from the selections. Since the rations were distributed in block form, the *"blockovas,"* the block leaders, mostly Jewish and Slovak women, divided the daily rations according to the number of prisoners in the block. Of course such division occurred after the *blockovas,* together with the *stubovas,* had skimmed off a big share for themselves.

The *stubovas* pushed us into the block and screamed: "find a *Koje"*, the name for the bunks. How ironic that it was the same name for a room on a cruise or passenger ship and yet given to these unspeakable abodes! I was lucky enough to be told by one of the *stubovas* to get a place on a top bunk. How right she was. At night, when of course no one was allowed to go to the latrine, located behind the last of the three new-arrival stone blocks, several buckets were placed outside the block entrance. The night guard, one of the *stubovas,* would watch over them and empty them into the latrine if they were full. She was not inclined to empty them too often, so when a prisoner would come out to use the bucket, and they were all almost full, the *stubova* had a stout stick and you would get the stick over your backside with the comment "*Marmeladenkopf* ("jelly head" one of the milder epithets) get back on your *Koje*." Well, what did one do in this case? One used the bowl in which to eliminate wastes. And of course after one used it, one had to get rid of the contents. Each bunk was built on two stout beams, anchored between two low stone walls. There was a small space between the walls and the boards on top of the beams. That was the space the bowl was emptied into. If you were located in the middle bunk, you got the contents into your bunk. That was my first lesson of survival in Birkenau.

Chapter Six

The Second Day in Birkenau

I will not burden the reader with a day-to-day description of my stay at Birkenau. However, I feel that the first two days, when the introduction to the deepest circle of Dante's Inferno become reality, need to be specifically described. As time went on, even the lowest of the prisoners, those on the *Aussenkommando,* the work-crews that went outside the camp to do heavy work without any tools and therefore destined for early gassing, became used to the daily routine that we were introduced to on the second day, provided of course, that they had made a conscious decision to try to stay alive however they could.

On the morning of the second day, it must have been 4:30 A.M. or so, shrill whistles sounded throughout the camp, and the block: *"Stavaite!"* *"Aufstehen!"* *"Stavat!"*--the three languages of the camp, Polish, German, Slovakian--dinned into our ears. The few lights in the block were turned on, and of course one tried to get to the latrine. Not everyone managed to get there in time which resulted in the soiling and wetting of the uniform we wore, never to be changed or washed, except on the rare occasion of a general delousing. Even then, since the rags were only gassed for delousing, the stench and filth accumulated on the body and the clothing. We might not get our own clothes back, but they all stank alike and were stiff with filth.

On the way to the latrine, some women tried to relieve themselves at the side of the road, but God help you if a *stubova* caught you; that would be the first beating you would receive. Yes, the *stubovas*, prisoners themselves, were quite ruthless with the newcomers. They had survived what they considered much worse times since the middle of 1942, and now they had power over the inexperienced new arrivals who needed to be disciplined to the camp life. Besides that, the *stubovas* spent the night on their individual "*Kojes,*" never more than two to a *Koje*, and they were not hungry, cold and exhausted like the new arrivals. The newcomers, on the other hand, had spent several days on the train, one night in the quarantine barracks, one day being processed in in the Sauna, and the first of many nights to come on the *Koje* with four or five other women. Hunger and exhaustion and horror of the unbelievable situation began to take their toll almost immediately. Thus, when a *stubova* would chase after a woman who tried to relieve herself before she reached the Sauna, it was no contest; the *stubova* would win the race and the beating would start.

Since there was only one faucet in the whole latrine, it was impossible for most of us to wash so we had to improvise if we were clearheaded enough to think of some way to wash what little showed of us, face and hands. The rest of our body we never exposed, if we could help it; there was no way to wash it anyway. One of the most effective ways for the

Nazis to demoralize us was to guarantee that we were kept as filthy as possible, thus making us feel less human and losing our will to resist and survive. Fleas, lice and bedbugs assailed the newcomers immediately, and there was no possible way to get rid of them. As already mentioned, not even the general delousing would do anymore than render the vermin unconscious and they would revive the minute they were on someone's body again.

As a substitute for washing with water we used the so-called coffee that was brought into the block after reveille, large kettles filled with a black liquid. We lined up to fill our bowls, but if we had used the bowl overnight to relieve ourselves, we had better have rinsed it out first, if we got the chance. Then we drank as much as we could, because any other source of drinking water, like the faucet in the latrine, was invariably contaminated with typhus bacteria. That was another service the *stubovas* rendered the new arrivals. They did warn us of the contaminated water.

The hot black water that passed for coffee or tea, whatever they called it, was the only other source of drinking water for the newcomers; water during the day, from the outside, was unavailable. During the first few days we learned to wash our hands and faces with the black water. We were warned by the *stubovas* that during the selections taking place every morning and every night, a dirty face or dirty hands could mean being taken out to the gas.

The "selections," on the same order that had taken place at the arrival ramp, took place every morning when the work details marched out to their work places, and again every night when they came back in. It was my impression that the main objective of the selections was to weed out the ill and exhausted-looking prisoners. The sadistic Germans having deprived us of all means of keeping ourselves clean had found the perfect trick to select their victims: clean hands and clean face, or you are "OUT." How we kept ourselves clean without any means of washing was not their concern. Lesson Two was being learned: keep hands and face clean; if we were too exhausted to do that, then we were ready for the gas.

I don't remember if we had been given any rations that first night, but I don't think so. Ergo we had only the black liquid to start the day. Not too long after the wake-up whistle came the whistle for *"Zählappell,"* roll-call, another typical Nazi institution of torment. The administration was determined to have its records of the body count every morning; how many alive, how many dead, how many diseased, how many detached on special assignment. Special assignment meant, for instance, women who worked in the Auschwitz camp or worked in the factories on nightshifts, or worked in the Hygiene Department, or the agriculture department, but still had to be counted in the women's camp roll call. Supposedly, according to Zippi Tichauer, who was the head of the *"Zeichenstube,"* the graphics department in the women's camp, the

124

count served mainly to make sure that enough food rations were prepared for the day.[1] That, of course, was rather deceptive, because, as the rations were delivered in bulk to the individual blocks, the *blockovas* and the *stubovas* skimmed off their share before distributing them. Therefore, lesson three we learned was to be sure and take our bowl with us, since that would hold your "soup" given to us for lunch on the *Aussenkommando*.

For the roll call we lined up in rows of five in front of the block; that procedure occurred daily, come rain or shine, or snow, heat or freezing temperatures. And we stood and stood. I have seen women simply lie down and die during the roll call. If that happened anywhere the counting had to start anew of course; we couldn't be one "dirty Jewess" short. And so we stood until the count was completed, recorded and tallied. God forbid, one prisoner might be hiding in the block, or perhaps too sick to get out of her bunk. Maybe she was ready to die her

---

[1] Unpublished ms. Zippi Tichauer, July, 1991.

own death. But that privilege was not given to any of us. It had to be a bureaucratically provoked and a bureaucratically recorded death. We would stand as close together in each row, trying to get some warmth from the woman in front of us and warm her back while the one behind us warmed ours.

After the roll call finally tallied, and it could take hours on end for it to do so, the *Aussenkommando Kapos* (outside work detail overseers) came around to literally shanghai the required amount of prisoners for their respective *Kommandos*. One had to learn quickly which of the *Aussenkommandos* was the worst and which the most endurable; which had a decent *Kapo*[2] where work was bearable. These *Aussenkommandos* were the assignments that were calculated to lead to the prisoner's death within approximately two months. The amount of

---

[2] *"Kapos"* were, with a few exceptions, mostly German or Polish criminals or politicals, who had been made the foreperson of a work detail, male or female. They had fairly unlimited power over the prisoners in their detail, and could use that power for good or evil.

126

calories given as daily nutrition were so minimal in comparison to the calories expanded on the work assignments on the outside that the body would eat its own fat in approximately that time. That was another one of the carefully calculated processes to speed up the descent to the gas chamber.[3]

One learned quickly which *Kapo* to avoid and which one to seek. All *Aussenkommando Kapos* were German women who had been convicted of crimes or acts considered crimes by the Nazis before coming to Birkenau. Those with black triangles in front of their numbers on their clothing were designated antisocial persons, such as prostitutes and bar-girls. Or they wore

---

[3] The Wannsee Konferenz, called by Reinhold Heydrich, the head of the Security Department in charge of the "Final Solution," took place in a villa outside of Berlin on the Wannsee, on January 20, 1942. A group of high-ranking SS administrators, 11 PhD's among them, decided in the 87- minute conference plans for the "Final Solution" and among other things, the dehumanization of the prisoners not only to speed their debilitation but to make it all the easier on the SS personnel to disregard any humanity in these prisoners. The less they looked like human beings, the easier for the SS to unhesitatingly maltreat and kill them.

green triangles, designating criminals and red triangles, designating political prisoners. To us, those who had the black triangles were preferable to those who had the green ones who were noted for their cruelty and viciousness. A number of the women who wore the black triangles were even somewhat human. These German women, numbering 1000, had been the first women sent to Auschwitz from Ravensbrück, in order to organize a planned women's camp.

After having been assigned to a work-detail we marched out, down the camp street, where we saw for the first time in daylight the whole other side of the camp. There sat the pre-fab blocks that housed the non-Jewish prisoners. They looked so clean and airy. We could not help but envy their treatment, so different from ours. As we neared the gate where the prisoner women's orchestra was playing the rousing German marches, which they did grotesquely whenever we walked in and out of the camp, and to which we had to keep

128

time,[4] there were the two SS-men again, the doctor and the non-commissioned one, the work-commando leader. Don't ask me what prompted me to do it--was it sheer stupidity, or simply ignorance of the rules?-- but I stepped out of my row of five-- I was on the outside edge, where the SS-men watched-- stood at attention and said to the SS-men: *"Melde gehorsamst Ich bin eine Bureaukraft"* ("With your permission I would like to report that I am an office worker.") I had addressed myself to the non-commissioned SS-man, probably figuring that the doctor would not be too interested in an office worker. For a moment the man stood there open-mouthed and

---

[4] The women's orchestra was established with the help of Polish men from the orchestra in Birkenau's men camp. The first conductor was a woman by the name of Tchaikowska. "Her name impressed the German's tremendously." In 1943 Alma Rosé, the daughter of the head of the famous Rosé Quartet, and a niece of Gustav Mahler, was brought to Birkenau. The block leader of the quarantine informed the central office of her arrival before Alma Rosé could be sent as a guinea pig to the experimental block. Alma was immediately transferred to Birkenau, made conductor of the orchestra and Tchaikowska was kicked upstairs as *blockova* of the musicians' block. The initial charge of the orchestra was to play for the marching out and in of the work details. Unpublished ms, Zippi Tichauer, July, 1991.

then he laughed and wrote down my number. I suppose I must still have looked like a human being, in spite of the bald head with kerchief and the uniform, since we just had arrived the day before, so perhaps that was the reason that he seemed to remember me throughout my stay in Birkenau.

Only later was I told that what I had done could have just as easily bought me a trip to the gas chamber. It just was not done to draw attention to oneself, but how was I to know? In Theresienstadt we were allowed to apply for a job and I assumed the same might hold true here. As we slowly marched past the two men they would ever so often use the crook of the canes they were holding to hook a prisoner's neck with and pull her out of the column to the side. There were already several women standing there, as we marched by. Since we were a brand new group, we did not seem to fit the criteria for the gas. We found out all too soon what these criteria were: shuffling feet, dirty hands and face, kerchiefs not tied correctly behind the head , apathetic gaze, scabies scars and, of course hunger oedema and skeletal appearance: a face that was no more than bones, a prominent nose, and big eyes with an empty gaze.

I really don't remember what the assignment of that first day was on the *Aussenkommando*. I only remember that we received "soup" brought out in the same type of large kettle that the coffee had been brought in. It consisted of lots of liquid with a very strange taste. I was told that the soup probably contained bromide to suppress the sexual drive. Prisoners assigned to the *Aussenkommandos* very quickly lost any sexual drive anyway, while their physical condition deteriorated. The good thing about that was that the bromide, it may be assumed, also stopped menstruation.

The soup had some weeds, and perhaps from time to time pieces of potatoes in the bottom. Therefore, the next survival lesson I learned was that when lining up for the soup in the *Aussenkommando* one should stand either well back, so that one might get a ladle full of the thicker stuff, or get in the good graces of the *Kapo,* who might just dip the ladle extra deep for you, so you would get some substance in the watery liquid. But on the first day we all almost gagged on the soup which a few weeks later was accepted greedily since in such a situation, one could get used to almost any kind of nourishment, distasteful as it was.

When we marched back into the camp, there was another selection with the same procedure. Upon questioning the *stubovas,* we were told in no uncertain terms what was happening to the women who were pulled out of the marching column. They were taken to block 25, the so-called death-block. The victims were collected from the morning and the evening selections. After curfew had been whistled throughout the camp, the trucks would drive up and load up the daily harvest of human beings to take them to the gas. They all knew where they were going and they did not go quietly. The most heart-rending of these transports I witnessed

Christmas Eve 1943, when the office work-detail, to which I belonged at the time, was assembled in the Sauna.

The SS had decided the office needed a Christmas party, so they had sent one of us with a guard out to cut a little tree. We, the office workers, made chains out of colored paper we had and the work detail assembled in the Sauna, with the orchestra. We sang Christmas carols, while the orchestra played them. At the same time a convoy of several trucks loaded with women destined to die drove down the road to the crematorium, right behind the Sauna. Neither our singing nor the orchestra was loud enough to drown out the cries, prayers and curses of the doomed women. Thus the Third Reich celebrated Christmas, the holiest day in Christendom, in Birkenau, 1943.

Several times in my two-year stay in Birkenau luck seemed to have a hand in my survival. I do not call it God watching over me, as I have read in so many survivor accounts, because I would consider it extremely presumptuous to assume that a God who could let thousands die every week in clouds of gas and flames in the crematorium would have selected me from the masses to lend a helping hand. Fate and luck are both capricious entities, and one of them interfered in my life soon after my arrival in Birkenau.

It seems that my foolhardy self-introduction to the SS-man during the marching out on the first day did not have negative results. On the contrary, the SS-man, who, it turned out was the *Arbeitsdienstführer* (the official in charge of labor assignments), must have given my number to the prisoner *Arbeitseinsatz* (prisoner labor assignment office), because a few days later after I had volunteered my services my number and several others from the new transport were called and we were told not to march out the next day. My friend, Lilly, my roommate from Theresienstadt, who was also in my block, was called as well. Lilly had been sent with one transport earlier, the one I had managed to stay out of. By the time of my arrival, which really was only a few days after hers, she already was showing signs of deterioration. Obviously in her case, it did not take more than a few days to begin the process of decline towards the inevitable road to the gas chamber.

Those of us who had been told to stay in the block after the roll call were taken again to the Sauna, but this time for a real hot shower. Then we were given the gray and blue camp dresses and three-quarter jackets without lining, which were made out of the same material. To this day I believe that the main ingredient of that fabric was wood. The clothes were hard and rough to the touch. If we had only clogs, we were given shoes. Then we were marched to Auschwitz I, the main camp, the KZ, the concentration camp, to distinguish it from the death camp Birkenau. The Nazis themselves called Birkenau *"Vernichtungslager"* (extermination camp). The term "Auschwitz," in the case of what was actually going on in this camp, was far less accurate than the name

"Birkenau" to symbolize the "Final Solution."
Over the gate in Auschwitz, like over all KZ
gates, was the legend *"Arbeit macht frei"* ("Work
makes you free."). No such legend was written
over the gate-tower in Birkenau. We were never
to be free.

We were led to one of the barracks
outside the main gate. The barracks housed the
offices of the *Stabsgebäude* (staff building of
Auschwitz-Birkenau). We were told that the
barracks we were in was the office of the
Politische Abteilung (literally Political
Department, but actually the Gestapo
headquarters). I don't know how many
interrogation rooms there were. I was put into
one of them, set in front of a typewriter and told
to type the transcript of the interrogation of a
prisoner in the room. He might have been a
civilian who had been caught as part of a
resistance group, a black marketeer or someone
under suspicion for some activity considered a
crime by the Nazis. He could just as well have
been innocent of anything and had been

denounced by someone who had a grudge against him. If he were an inmate of the camp, he would have been accused of smuggling a letter to the outside, or having been discovered in an escape plot or a conspiracy with other political prisoners.

I just remember typing furiously all day long, being dictated to by the SS what should be in the record, not thinking, working almost mechanically. I tried to tune out the cries of the prisoner as he was being put on the "Boger Swing," the contraption that would hang him upside down, tied together by his hands and feet, and have his exposed rear end beaten mercilessly. As one of the defendants in Peter Weiss's play The Investigation says: "The beating would stop if the blood soaked through the prisoner's pants."[5] There must have been more than one interrogation during that day. At the end of the day, we, who had hoped to be kept there, warm and clean at least for a few

---

[5] Peter Weiss, The Investigation. English translation by Jon Swan and Ulu Grosbard. New York: Atheneum, p.87.

days, were marched back to Birkenau because it seemed one of our group was found to have a high fever and symptoms of typhus. So it was back to Birkenau to what seemed further days of the *Aussenkommando*, until we would be ready for the gas.

As a matter of fact, it was a few days after that when Lilly said to me: " I am going to block 27." Block 27 was the only Jewish hospital block in the camp. There were at least nine more hospital blocks on the Aryan side, forming the so-called *"Krankenbau."* Block 27 was run, more or less, by a French physician called Doctor Rose. Since I never was in the hospital block, I don't know to this day if this was her first name or her family name. But since all of us only had numbers, and if we lived long enough were known only by our first name, I assume it was her first name.

On the Jewish side there was no need for more hospital blocks. Anyone who entered "the hospital" did not really receive any treatment. The SS-doctor of the day would walk at least once a day through Block 27 and pull those prisoners out of the bunk who looked ready for the gas, in his opinion, and most of them were. That is the block Lilly wanted to go to. I tried to dissuade her, but she repeated over and over again: "This is no way to live, I don't want to live this way." She went to Block 27, accompanied by the *blockova*, and when I inquired after her at Block 27, the next day, between marching in from the *Aussenkommando* and camp curfew, she was gone.

After about a week on the *Aussenkommando* I think, I was told once more to stay in the block after roll call. And once more I was taken to the Sauna, this time by myself, showered, got my head freshly shaved, got fresh clothes and I believe even "new" shoes, not new, that is, but better than the ill-fitting ones I had gotten at the time of the processing-in. I could not help wondering if this special treatment was due still to the influence of the *Arbeitsdienstführer* who kept remembering the foolhardy prisoner who dared to address him while stepping out of the marching- out formation. Or perhaps my typing had made an impression on the SS man for whom I had typed the transcript for the interrogations that had promoted me to the *Stabsgebäude*, this time as a full-fledged member of the *Politische Abteilung* work detail.

That work-detail did all the administrative work for the entire camp-complex, Auschwitz I, the concentration camp, Auschwitz II, Birkenau and Auschwitz III the factory sub-camps near Birkenau. We were all housed in the basement of the *Stabsgebäude,* the staff building of the main camp, located right outside the gate of Auschwitz I. Until 1993, when I visited Auschwitz with my children, I had never set foot inside the main camp.

The *Politische Abteilung* prisoners worked either as private secretaries to the leading SS-men, or worked in the so-called *Standesamt* (bridal registry office). That must have been one of the many cynical jokes of the SS, because no one ever got married in that *Standesamt.* On the contrary, all deaths were registered there, whether by gas or other means. There were other women workers living in the basement: the sewing room work unit, the laundry work unit, and perhaps some other good work details, because by camp standards, the *Stabsgebäude* basement was the Ritz, with bed linens, clean bathrooms, and heated rooms. I was assigned to one of the dormitories in the basement.

The first person speaking to me there was Dagmar Ostermann, then Dagmar Bock, a Viennese girl, who became my protectress of sorts during the time I was there. To this day I have remained in touch with her as one of my best friends. Dagmar had been in Auschwitz since 1942 and had had the good fortune to be almost immediately assigned to the *Stabsgebäude*. Of course, by February 1943 she was already an "old prisoner." She had been fortunate to be interned as a "political prisoner" and not a *"Schutzhäftling"* like all of us Jews who had been deported into the camp from a collection point. She was also a *"Mischling,"* only half Jewish. Since the issue of the Nuremberg race laws in 1935, Jews were designated as either full Jews or mixed "breeds" of different gradations, quarter, half or three quarter mixes. Most of the mixed "breeds" were usually the result of mixed marriages, and if the children had been raised non-Jewish, they were allowed to live as almost Aryans. There were records of mixed "breeds" even in the German Army. A German General by the name of Milch was known to be of Jewish descent. Reinhard Heydrich, the infamous head of security, was said to be so supervicious against Jews in order to live down the fact that he had a Jewish grandmother or great grandmother.

It seems to me that the relatively short time that I was in the *Stabsgebäude* remained more or less a blur, except for the beginning and the end. I remember being interviewed by *Rottenführer* Perry Broad, an SS man with an American father and a German actress mother. I believe he told me all that during the interview. It must have been the first day after arriving there that I was sent to be interviewed for placement by him. At the time I did not know the typical Auschwitz regulation of demeaning the prisoner by forcing him or her to stand at attention not less than one or two meters distance from any SS man. Perhaps that rule was partly instituted for fear of contamination with all of the diseases that were running rampant in the camps, or perhaps it was just one more of the demeaning chicaneries of the Nazis. I started to sit down in the chair in front of his desk. He told me in strict but not unfriendly terms about the standing rule. I don't remember how we got to the fact that he spoke fluent English and that he was a jazz fan. It was probably the most normal conversation he had held with a prisoner who was to be interviewed and the conversation we had must have stuck in his mind, in spite of the thousands of prisoners he encountered between February 1943 and October 1944, when we met again under strange circumstances which I will discuss later.

Broad assigned me to work for SS-man Boger, he of the famous "Boger Swing," one of the most notoriously vicious Gestapo members of Auschwitz. However, he did not use me for interrogation writing anymore. I did not have very much to do, and if I was totally idle, I was sent to the "*Standesamt*," the large office, where every death in the camp was recorded, not the ones that went directly into the gas from the ramp, but anyone with a number, whether Jew or Aryan political prisoner. About twenty girls were regularly working in that large room, but they could always use an extra hand, because they were incredibly busy recording the daily deaths in the camp.

Unfortunately, that almost-haven of security by Birkenau standards did not last very long for me. One day I was told that I and two sisters from Saarbrücken, the last three prisoners added to the work unit, would be sent back to Birkenau. It seems one of the women in the *Stabsgebäude*, to this day I don't know from which of these units, had been caught passing a letter to a male prisoner. Not that that was not done all the time, but when someone was caught, the punishment was collective. I don't remember what happened to the woman; she was probably assigned to a punishment work unit in Birkenau. The punishment work unit was usually reserved for Aryan prisoners. Jews were sent to the gas for any infringement of the rules. A punishment work unit was a type of *Aussenkommando,* with hard work and minimal living conditions. Most of the punishment detail had, of course, been administrative workers or workers in good positions, which made the punishment commando all the harder for them. Unfortunately for me, an example was made for the whole *Stabsgebäude* for that infringement of the rules by transferring the last ones brought in back to Birkenau. Neither Dagmar nor anyone else could help, and I knew that I would now experience the true unending horror of Birkenau. The time was March of 1943.

Chapter Seven

Birkenau Revisited

The return to Birkenau, brief as my stay in the *Stabsgebäude* had been, was of course traumatic: out of the relatively clean basement of the *Stabsgebäude* with indoor toilets and wash facilities to the stone blocks and their *"Kojen"* and the hundreds of women in the block. When we returned in March, B1a was still the women's camp, separated from B1b, the men's camp, by a fence. The three of us who had been sent back from the *Stabsgebäude* were stuck into Block 3 of B1a. Somehow I lost sight of the two sisters and never saw them again.

One of the first lessons for survival, in the women's camp at least, was to find a "group." You could not designate them with the now-so-prevalent word "family." "Support group" would be the closest to modern terminology. Support for survival was the main interest of such groups in the new-arrival blocks, the women thrown together on a common *"Koje."* And we would look out for each other. When one member of the group developed typhoid fever, or the gastroenteritis so prevalent in the camp, the rest of us would share the rations she could not use, and prepare for her the only medication that was available for these diseases short of going to Block 27 to certain death: charcoaled bread. To this day, natural charcoal is probably the best cure for an upset stomach, only we are so used to medications and prescriptions that we never think of natural remedies.

In terms of rations, what was given to us, the carefully calculated rations that debilitated the prisoner so that she could be more quickly readied for selection to the gas, consisted of the following:

In the morning the so-called coffee or tea, hot colored liquid, with hardly any taste, but at least we knew that it was probably boiled so as not to contain disease-carrying bacteria. At noon, on whatever work detail we were on outside, the kettle was brought to us. The so-called soup was handed out by the *Kapo*. One tried not to be the first one in line because the ration coming from the top of the kettle was mostly water. Farther down was the "thick" stuff: potato peels, turnips, weeds, and other scraps. Nothing very nourishing, certainly. It was the smell of the turnips that seemed to permeate the entire *Aussenkommando* population. We all stank from it, and it soaked through our skin it would seem, the skin that never had a chance to be washed, and the clothes that never had a chance to be changed. In the evening upon returning from the *Aussenkommando* and after standing for roll call again, we received a piece of bread, 6" long by 4" wide by 3" thick. I could swear it was mostly sawdust. Once a week we received a slice of sausage, maybe 1/3" thick, once a week a little square of margarine, and once a week a dab of beetroot marmalade. The office workers, and the better *Kommandos*, would every so often receive what was known as *"Zulage"*: extra rations, like perhaps a potato in the peel, or a teaspoonful of sugar.

One tried not to eat the bread all at once, to leave a little piece at least for the morning. But it was very difficult without a knife. After all, everything was done with the fingers, and until one survived long enough to get into an inside job with housing in a different block where one could perhaps, for a bread ration, buy a knife, and/or a spoon, it was the fingers for us.

To get off the *Aussenkommando* and into a job that allowed one NOT to have to go through the daily morning and night selections at the gate, again one followed the unwritten rules, so prevalent in the women's camp (I do not know anything about such rules in the men's camp.). To find the job "inside the fence" one had to find a connection, either someone who had a job on the inside, or someone who might know you from the life you led before you had been put into the camp. Those in position of assigning jobs had the obligation to help such a person on the *Aussenkommando* if the person had the possibility to get in touch with her. That, of course, was again a problem, because most women with an inside job lived in blocks assigned to their work detail and would most of the time avoid contacts with new arrivals, mainly because of the danger of contamination from the prevalent highly contagious diseases these women would get such as typhus, scarlet fever, gastroenteritis, or jaundice. Unless you were selected at the ramp because of your profession, such as doctors and pharmacists, you had to find out as soon as possible about the rule of connections and find your connections for an "inside " job, even if that job meant carrying corpses, cleaning latrines, or sweeping the camp streets.

The things I remember from those months in Block 3 are like images, nothing in sequence. I managed to become a member of a group, the absolute necessity for survival. My group, my "*Koje*" mates, since I was in a new arrival block of mostly German and French Jewish women, was what at the time I considered to be a number of older women. They must have been between 35 and 45. It was, of course, unusual for women of that age not to be sent to the gas, but I found out why this particular group, about four, possibly five of them, had escaped such treatment: they had been married to non-Jewish men. The men had either voluntarily or under compulsion, divorced the women, and the minute these women were divorced they became eligible like any other Jewish person to be deported in 1943. I think they were from Berlin, if I remember correctly, but as I said, my memory of that time is erratic. I really feel ashamed that I cannot recall a single name of any of the women, because they basically saved my life. Perhaps I am blotting out some memories of the Block 3 period because it was the time of my closest brush with death.

Not long after returning from the *Stabsgebäude*, I began running the dreaded fever, the first sign of typhus, a disease spread by lice. Gastroenteritis followed. As I described above, the group would take the rations I could not eat for themselves and would feed me all the charcoaled bread I could keep down. Of course toasting the bread meant standing in line because so many people needed the charcoaled bread. Every morning for roll call, I would stand between two of the women and they would practically hold me up. I suppose they must have managed to get me into the same *Aussenkommando* that they were recruited in because I remember them practically carrying me through the selection that at that time took place every morning and every night.

I certainly looked like a *Muselmann*: concave in places were female bodies were supposed to be convex, with big eyes and a long nose in a skeleton face. But I distinctly recall keeping my eyes wide open and trying for what must have been a hideous grin to prove that I was not the apathetic, shuffling, *Muselmann*, ready for the gas.

I also recall that on one of the *Aussenkommando* details the *Kapo* must have been somewhat kind, because my group seemed to have managed to deposit me behind a part of a ruined house. We were tearing down bombed out buildings. I remember finding and eating *Sauerampfer* (sorrel) which had a wonderful refreshing taste. I don't know what it would taste like today, but at that time, when it was almost impossible for me to get anything down but the charcoaled toast, it was like tasting a delicacy. I don't know for how many days my group dragged me through the selection, but one evening the *blockova*, Ilka Grün, who had (somewhat) befriended me as much as such a thing as kindness was possible, since I was the only one in the block who spoke Czech, and could easily communicate with her, who was Slovak, said: "Susan tomorrow you must go to Block 27 (hospital block); I can't keep you in the block any longer." I begged her to give me one more day resting in our block, and if after that one day I was not better, I would go to Block 27. Ilka agreed and the next morning I stayed in the block. I stood in roll call with the help of my group and then was allowed back into the block. Ilka gave me one vitamin C tablet and one aspirin. I suppose I grabbed at anything that looked like medication from the world outside; I believed it would help me. Strange to say, the miracle did happen.

I still remember distinctly that lying in the bunk by myself, my head toward the outer edge to catch some air, I suddenly had a strange feeling, as if the bottom of the bunk were falling away from under me and there was a void beneath me. I grabbed the edge of the bunk with both hands and gripped as hard as I could and slowly it seemed as if the bottom of the bunk was coming up again under me. When I loosened my grip from the edge, my fingernails, what there was of them, were torn and bloody. When I took my children to Birkenau in 1993, that bunk in Block 3 was still there.

Miraculously, that moment on that day must have been the crisis point in my disease. The next morning I awoke with a renewed feeling of strength and no fever. I managed to march out, of course with the help of my group, but things were improving for me. Was that some kind of a instinctive life force asserting itself, and were there so many who could not call upon it? After having overcome the typhus and gastroenteritis, I began to turn very yellow, and remember a feeling like I had a stone in my stomach. What little food there was I could not eat: I had jaundice. I must assume that whatever food there was available did not contain anything that would aggravate jaundice and I did turn white again, but to this day I am disqualified as a blood donor.

One Sunday I suppose they were cleaning out the block and had chased us all outside to the empty space between blocks two and three. On Sundays everyone tried to do some cleaning; the *stubovas* and even the outside workers were still women who had the basic feminine instinct of some kind of order. We were allowed out of the block on Sundays during the day. Sometimes there were even concerts by the women's orchestra on the camp street. That particular day was a beautiful spring day. Of course there was nothing green for us to look at--there was nothing green in Birkenau with the exception of weeds; behind and in front of the blocks the ground was simply trampled down. A few weeds might rear their timid heads, but nothing more than that. The sun was shining strong enough, so I suppose it must have been May, 1943. I was sitting on the hard ground, and I had taken off my uniform jacket. I distinctly remember thinking: "Things cannot be absolutely bad; I still can take a sunbath." How ridiculously unrealistic could I get? I almost forgot about the other side of that coin, how really incredibly cruel and bad things could be.

An illustration of that point is a memory from March, 1943, shortly after I returned from the *Stabsgebäude*. There was one day of "General Delousing." All our clothes were taken from us. Anything that we might have acquired through bartering with our precious rations like a scarf, a knife, a spoon, was gone. The population of the entire women's camp stood naked outside in front of the gate practically all day and it was still bitter cold, perhaps the beginning of, or mid-March.

How many died that day I don't know, I believe I contracted my typhus fever at that time, being weakened and cold. It was probably my luck that I still had enough resistance left until that time, by having been in the *Stabsgebäude* shortly after my arrival and not having gone through the usual horrors of new arrivals. I remember, however, distinctly that moving back into camp was of course combined with another selection. As we stood outside of the camp gate on the open field, we had to run back into the camp through the selection. And the SS-man in charge had invented a new game. We had to run and he held his walking stick a certain height. If we could not jump over it, it was the gas for us.

During this period, while being assigned to the various outside details, I once was very "lucky" to be assigned to the *"Weisskäppchen,"* a rag-sorting detail within the camp's confines. It was in a barrack, which meant I was able to be relatively warm and mainly dry. It must have been around that time that I acquired the only visible scar of my Birkenau period. I vaguely remember that it was during a line-up waiting for the noon-time soup. I must have shoved someone, or have been shoved, but I do distinctly remember a female *Kapo* coming down the line and hitting me with a club over the head. Today, from time to time, my beautician will say, "I found the hole in your head." Not exactly a hole, but a noticeable indentation on the right side of my skull. (By the way, the *"Kanada"* work detail had a second name, probably given to it by a cynical SS-man. It was called *"Rotkäppchen" Kommando* because of the red kerchiefs worn by the women of the detail. *"Rotkäppchen"* translates into "Little Red Riding Hood," which, considering the situation, was a grisly irony).

In the *Stabsgebäude* among other women, was one girl, I cannot remember her name, who befriended me. When I was so unceremoniously dismissed back to Birkenau, she said that she would contact her sister, who was a *Läuferin*. This was a liaison runner between the administrative office and the blocks. There was no telephone connection between the blocks and the *Schreibstube* which was the administrative block of the women's camp. She would let her know that I was from Prague because it seemed her sister had lived in Prague for a while. The unwritten law about people in positions helping *Aussenkommando* women if they had any connection with them through direct or indirect acquaintance applied in this case.

This contact was my literal salvation. I had mentioned that Ilka Grün, the *blockova,* liked me; she was the one that gave me the day's grace that helped me to survive. From time to time I would help Ilka with interpreting, since her German was weak, and her French non-existent, and in addition to German speakers there were also some French women in the block. It was one day in her little block chamber, the space reserved for the *blockovas* in each block, that I met the sister of the girl from the

Stabsgebäude. Her sister must have given her my number, and she, being in the administrative office, had no trouble in finding the number. It had, however, taken almost three months for her to get to me. I suppose I must have been just one of many women whom she was trying to help. Talking to her it came out that not only was she familiar with Prague, but also one of my best gentile friends in Prague, a newspaper reporter by the name of Jimmy, was also a good friend of hers. I suppose that put me one rung higher in her list of those needing help.

She got me a transfer to the administrative work detail. I was, of course, overjoyed because that could mean life for a while at least instead of certain death. But it also meant saying good-bye to my group. Being transferred out of the new -arrival block into an elite detail block like the *Schreibstube* (administrative office) meant that I could not communicate anymore or have direct contact with anyone from the new-arrival block. The danger of contamination from one of the many diseases being allowed by the Nazis to run rampant in the camp for the express purpose of infecting more of their victims was too great to risk a visit. I do not remember the name of any of these kind women. I hope they survived since they were political prisoners who had come into the camp with a file meaning that, though they were Jews, they could not be gassed. They had the privilege of dying their own death.

It was then that I had learned another lesson the hard way: do not get too attached to anyone or to anything in the form of possessions. It and they could disappear in a flash, be it through selections, through delousing, through death. Was that also part of the psychological cruelties devised by the very clever psychologists of the Nazis? Make people, even in secure positions, as insecure as possible. Was the whim of the SS the only thing one could count on?

Chapter Eight
Schreibstube

According to Danuta Czech's *Calendarium* I came into the *Schreibstube* in July, 1943, after the opening of B1b, as the second part of the women's camp, because I was transferred to the *Schreibstube,* Block 4 in B1b. It was once more like coming from hell to at least the lowest level of purgatory. I had survived probably the worst period of my camp time, from when I was sent back from the *Stabsgebäude* in March of 1943, until I was assigned to the *Schreibstube* in July 1943.

I was deloused in the Sauna, this time again with a real shower, and, of course, my head was shaved once more, and then probably sprayed or rubbed with some lotion that would kill the nits, the lice eggs still residing on my shaved head. The camp underwear, a shift and sort of boxer shorts, also blue and white stripes, were the first fresh garments I received since I had returned from the *Stabsgebäude*. The clothes I received back after the general delousing could not be counted as a fresh set of clothes because from such perfunctory mass delousings the fleas and lice were simply stunned and would awaken immediately to new life, as soon as the garment was on the prisoner.

I delighted in my clean clothes, the blue and white striped dress that went over the shift and boxer shorts, the black apron and a white kerchief, also shoes and stockings. I don't remember what they were, but I am sure I got them, because the *Schreibstube* had shoes and socks in the summer, unlike the outside details, who went barefoot during the summer.

The *Schreibstube* and the living quarters of the work detail were all in one block: the back one-third contained single three-tiered bunks, with straw sacks, and even blankets; the second section was the day-room with long tables and benches; and the front, housed on the left side, (coming in) the *Schreibstube*, the administrative

office, and on the right the graphic department and *Zeichenstube* (drafting office) where Zippi Spitzer reigned, and the private room of Katja Singer, the *Rapportschreiberin* (recording secretary), the highest-ranking Jewish prisoner in the woman's camp.
The *Schreibstube* was the nerve center of the women's camp. All the block reports and orders, whether coming through the SS or from the *Schreibstube* personnel, came from that center. All the organization of the women's camp had been developed by Zippi Spitzer, and Katja Singer[1]

---

[1]They developed the daily master sheet, which counted every woman in the camp area, wherever she was, the factory camps, the agricultural details, all the barracks in Bla and Blb, in the *Stabsgebäude,* in Budy, the agricultural camp, the night shift workers in the factories, in *Kanada* and in the SS canteen . Those outside of Birkenau were listed as "detached." The master sheet had debit and credit columns. Those on the nightshifts outside of the women's camp area were listed as "debits." The *Arbeitseinsatz,,* the prisoner labor department, had its own card index sorted by professions. The SS-labor department receiving requests from the factories or individuals in the camp organization for workers would work through the *Arbeitseinsatz* card index to fill the request for manual workers or professionals through the *Arbeitseinsatz.* Unpublished manuscript, Zippi Tichauer. July 1991.

Katja had not only a private room; she also had her own chamber maid who was called Pani Zosha. She made sure that Katja's clothes were ironed, her boots polished, and she would always have warm water for washing. Women from *Kanada*, the elite work detail, would supply Katja's wardrobe, and Katja had the power to show her appreciation by listening to requests for transfers, sometimes even rescues from the gas, hospital stays, and other such vital favors.

That was also part of camp life. If we wanted something done for ourselves or a friend or relative, we bought ourselves that favor with a gift, to whomever had the power to grant it. The *Kanada* work detail members were the only ones who really had the resources for such gift-giving, and they made sure that Katja was always well supplied with sweaters, pants, blouses, underwear, whatever was needed. This sounds obscene in the midst of the horror and deprivation in the women's camp, but that was the surrealistic world of Birkenau. If you were a long-time prisoner in any kind of position, mainly in the offices, the hospital blocks, or the kitchens, you could obtain almost anything from clothing to medication through your connections. And anyone in a "privileged" position had connections.

Even the lowly block workers had the chance to buy items with food. They took advantage of the opportunity to skim off the rations that were assigned to the blocks in bulk and supply themselves by paying with their "profits." It must be said, however, that quite a few women owed their lives to Katja's intervention, done at considerable personal risk. Between her and Zippi, the head of the *Zeichenstube*, with whom she had arrived from the *Patronka* in Slovakia, they did their best for their friends. It so happened that most of the friends they rescued were Slovakian girls, but that is understandable because such a small number was left from the original transports of thousands in 1942 that they wanted to be able to save this remnant.

Many a time Zippi would transfer a girl to the *Schreibstube* when she found out that that girl was ready for the next selection. The girl would sit in the *Schreibstube* and do some non-essential make-work that looked important. In case an SS-man would come into the *Zeichenstube*, the *Muselmann*, for by that time the girl that Zippi would save had been reduced to a *Muselmann* state, would try to look very busy and indispensable. All of us who were in any kind of position to help less fortunate prisoners on the outside did whatever we could. Katja and Zippi were in the best position to perform miracles of rescue from the gas. As for me, later, when I was in the *Kanada* work detail, I smuggled clothing for friends who would ask me to get them underwear, sweaters and other garments.

In the *Schreibstube* I was placed on one of the high stools in front of a big book into which I entered the names from a list of women who had been selected to be numbered and put into the camp. Those selected for the gas at the ramp never were registered. The only records for those thousands were found after the war in the transport lists kept by the SS from the various departure locations in the occupied countries.

There was another list, the result of the daily selections. I had to put a line through the names and numbers in the big book that appeared on that list. Any transfers from one workplace to another, or the hospital block, was, I believe, registered in the *Arbeitseinsatz*. They dealt with the activities of those who were still alive and working. It is not widely known, but many of the inmates of Auschwitz were "hired out" to businesses nearby by the day in order to make a profit for the SS who, in some respects, ran the camp like an employment agency from hell. It was only due to the need for workers by the German industries that Birkenau was not established on the same principle as the other five extermination camps already mentioned, an extermination location only, but rather as a combination labor-extermination camp.

The Germans ran short of skilled workers for their major war industries. Since German men were in the Army, slave labor from the occupied countries was hard to come by; such workers managed to hide from being inducted. Thus a successful bargain was concluded between the SS and the major industries of the country such as Mercedes-Benz, Volkswagen, Krupp, IG Farben and many of the industries that today represent the core of the thriving German industrial complex. The SS built factories around Auschwitz I and II. The area was given the name of a small nearby village, Monowitz, or Auschwitz III, where the workers selected from the transports would work until they were ready for the gas, and then there was only a short trip from Monowitz to Birkenau and the gas chambers. The profits were very satisfactory for both the SS and the employers.

When today I tell my students that I considered myself "lucky" to have been sent to Auschwitz-Birkenau, I get uncomprehending, horrified stares until I give them the above explanation.

Though I did not get any more food than the allocated rations, I began to lose the *Muselmann* look within a short time. Sitting and writing did not take quite the calories compared to the calories slaving on any of the outside details did. There were quite a few Polish Aryan girls in the *Schreibstube* and they would get big packages from home with all sorts of good things: sausages, cheese, cookies. The policy of the SS was to permit such privileges for the gentiles and deny it to the Jews, thus making the condition of those they wished to exterminate that much more wretched. It was agony just to smell the mouth-watering aromas coming from those packages. I always waited until the recipients were ready to throw the carton away and before they did, I would snatch the crumbs of whatever cakes or bread were left in the bottom of the carton.

Ironically enough I was transferred out of the *Schreibstube* detail because one of the Polish girls accused me of having stolen bread from her. God knows I never got more than the crumbs of anyone's bread. But my transfer reflected one of the unwritten laws of the women's camp. Once you were employed in an inside position, even the lowliest detail, such as the corpse-bearer detail, you could be dismissed out of the detail, but you would not be sent back to the outside. You might be demoted perhaps to a lower detail, such as the camp roads cleaning detail, or given a lateral promotion to perhaps the rag-picking detail *(Weisskäppchen)*, or even sometimes to a better detail. Whatever direction your transfer took, once in the inside workforce, you were relatively secure from the outside detail. My transfer could probably be called a lateral transfer. I therefore stayed in Block B 4, the *Schreibstube* block, because I was still considered administrative personnel.

Being in the *Schreibstube* did not mean that every one of our ills was cured. I had a bad case of scabies, a skin disease, which was a very dangerous disease to have if you were in the daily selections since that would be reason enough to be taken to the gas. Fortunately, the

Schreibstube work detail stood roll call in front of the block, and we were not included in the marching out where the selections took place. I don't know who gave me the advice of washing with urine to cure the scabies, but it worked. Since one did not dare to go for scabies remedy to the hospital block, even from the *Schreibstube,* I was very grateful for the advice.

In the beginning of September, 1943, the *"Familienlager"* was born.[2] It was located in sector BIIb. Men, women and children stayed together in that camp. They were allowed to keep their luggage, and their hair was not shaved. I remember standing at the gate to the Sauna, which was next door to Block 4, and seeing Ernstl Fuchs, my Theresienstadt boyfriend, come out of the Sauna. I managed to wave to him but that was as close as I dared to go. Within the next few weeks I wangled a trip with a food kettle detail to the family camp. I

---

[2]According to the chronicler, Zdenek Lederer, 5600 men, women and children arrived at Birkenau and were put into the "Family camp." Ghetto Theresienstadt,. p.251.

172

must have looked a fright to them with my short hair and my striped camp clothing. I assured all the friends that I saw how lucky they were to be together and have their own clothes. They did not realize what the rest of the camp looked like. I am sure they learned it pretty quickly.

Everyone there thought they were incredibly lucky until March of 1944 when in one night, the whole Theresienstadt *Familienlager,* except for a few hundred people, went into the gas. They had served their purpose to counteract rumors about the extermination camps making the rounds in the free world.[3]

After having been accused of stealing from the *Schreibstube* work detail, I was

---

[3] The Nazis had planned to use the Family Camp in Birkenau as a back-up, just in case the "Embellishment Program" in Theresienstadt did not satisfy the Red Cross inspection team. The second large transport from Theresienstadt to the Family Camp came in May 1944, shortly before the official Red Cross inspection in June of 1944. When the Swiss Inspector, Maurice Rossel, raved about the comforts and luxury of the Theresienstadt Ghetto there was no more need for the Family Camp, and all the people went into the gas in September of 1944. Ibid.

transferred to the *Bauleitung* (construction) detail. In this case I profited from the unwritten law in the women's camp that I explained above, namely, once you were in the administrative track, like *Schreibstube, Kanada, Kleiderkammer* (clothing warehouse), kitchen, post office, or orchestra, you could not be kicked back out into the outside work detail unless you had committed a deadly sin, like writing to the outside world without authorization or being caught with a man, or smoking. Other than for such "crimes," we would be horizontally transferred or kicked upstairs. Thus in November of 1943, although I was transferred to the *Bauleitung*, I remained in the administrative block and it was there, as I have already mentioned, that I experienced the unforgettable incongruity of Christmas carols being sung by the *Schreibstube* prisoners and played by the women's orchestra while being drowned out by the screams and prayers of a transport of women going to the gas on the holiest night of Christendom.

The women's orchestra in Birkenau was probably the best maintained, fed and housed detail in the entire women's camp. Their conductor, as previously noted, Alma Rosé, the daughter of the head of one of the most famous classical quartets in Europe, the Rosé Quartet, ran this orchestra as if there were no extermination camp on the outside of her block. She demanded daily rehearsals and performed many concerts for the SS hierarchy. They also played every morning for the marching out of all the details that worked outside of the camp, and played again their rousing German marches for the return of the workforce. I remember an outdoor concert given by the orchestra on a Sunday for all the women's camp prisoners (See p. 128, f.4.).

Chapter Nine

Bauleitung, Hospital

After having lectured so many times about my different positions in the camp, the one I never was completely honest about until now is the period in which I worked in the *Bauleitung.* A Yugoslavian girl and I were transferred from the *Schreibstube* to the *Bauleitung.* The Yugoslavian was blonde, tall, a recently arrived prisoner, in fairly good condition, no marks of starvation, or scabies, or the like. I, having just begun to emerge from the *Muselmann* state, was still always hungry and very insecure in the work detail where the two of us were the only females among the male prisoners that frequented the office. We typed specifications for future camps; they must have been planning to cover the entire area between the Polish-German border and I would say probably the Ural Mountain range with camps. Every nationality was destined to be included in the plans of the Thousand-Year

Reich. Nations would be either decimated and sterilized to be used as slaves, or exterminated as was planned for the Slavic nations, since they were considered by the Nazis to be definitely a subhuman species. Only the Scandinavian countries and the British were given the honor of surviving, because, of course, they were Nordic races, and therefore, probably a lot more "pure Aryan" than any German national, who ironically, belonged to a "mixed" race.

Germany is situated in the center of Europe: to the east Poland and the Czech area, to the north the Scandinavian countries, to the west the Dutch, the Belgians, the French, to the south the Swiss, the Austrians, the Hungarians. How could the Germans have stayed a "pure race?" The Great Migration marched through there from east to west and left God knows what "races" behind. Were there never any racial mixings across the borders? How did the propaganda minions of Joseph Goebbels really make the nation believe in its racial purity? However, enough of them must have been convinced to draw up the plans for the destruction or submission of all non-Aryans. Ilona, the Yugoslavian girl, and I, kept typing the future plans of the Third Reich. The men who worked in the work detail were mostly Polish craftsmen in their field, electricians, carpenters, and others skilled in construction. One called Zdiszek was very nice to me; he would bring me some bread every so often. But one had to be very careful in that work detail with any kind of contact. The head of the *Bauleitung*, *Sturmbannführer* Janisch, an Austrian Nazi with probably a Nazi pedigree back to the time of the illegal movement in Austria in the 20's, was a stickler for *Lager* (concentration camp) rules.

He once caught me with a cigarette butt and threatened to send me to the *Strafkommando* (the punishment detail) or to the gas. I admit that I begged for my life on my knees. I did not care how I behaved: pride was the farthest thing from my mind. I was determined to stay alive. I will never know what prompted Janisch to relent. Was his power-hunger satisfied with my groveling, or did he have an attack of pity?

Not only were we the typists; we also were the cleaning women. We had to scrub the barracks floor with cold water and a hard brush on our hands and knees. Janisch would watch us and make sure that not a spot remained on the wooden floor.

The *Kapo* of the men's *Bauleitung* detail was a German green triangle (habitual criminal) by the name of Jupp. Jupp was big, blond, well-nourished, and menacing. One day he invited me to come to the store room where he would give me some food from home. Starved as I was, and not daring to contradict that brute, I went. What followed was a plain quick rape on the floor of the store room and a bit of sausage thrown at me for payment. That I was a Jewess did not bother the pure Aryan superman, Jupp.[1]

---

[1] The Nuremberg Laws of 1935 pertaining to Aryan purity forbid sexual relations between Jews and "pure" Germans. The term was "*Rassenschande*" and if found out, the penalty could be severe for the Aryan as well as the Jew.

The racial laws did not apply to him; he was not in uniform, and he knew that I would not dare to complain anywhere because being a Jewish woman, with no power or secure connections, unlike Jupp who probably was a lifer and had been in camp for years, I would be the one going to the gas and he would not even be reprimanded.

It was not long after that that my genitals began to itch terribly, and I had a vaginal discharge. It did not take long until someone noticed my contortions to allay the itching. The *blockova* was informed and I was ordered with the whole work detail to the hospital block. We all had to undergo a gynecological examination. They took longer with me than with the others and I still can hear the voice of one of the prison doctors saying: *Ulceri non specificae* (non-specific ulceration).

I was transferred to the hospital compound and diagnosed with VD. I did not know what kind. Someone, I think one of the prison doctors, said syphilis; someone else said gonorrhea. I suppose Jupp had left me with a good dose of the clap. By that time the hospital compound, consisting of a number of pre-fab blocks, had been opened for Jewish prisoners and being one of the old numbers, I was put into a single bed way back in the block and did not have to worry about selections.

I saw myself already in the gas for having contracted the VD, though I was never asked about any contact with a man. I will never understand why not. It might have been the timing. By that time, in addition to the fact that the Aryan hospital block had been opened for Jewish prisoners, it was also a period of less transports and less selections.

It seems someone, I do not know who, must have informed Zdiszek, the nice Pole, of my condition. And a few days later he came to see me in the hospital block with a full dosage of Neosalvarsan ampules: Dr. Ehrlich's "magic bullet." Funny, when I read about Dr. Ehrlich's discovery in Paul De Kruif's book Microbe Hunters as a teenager in Vienna, I certainly could not have foreseen that his discovery would be so welcome to me. I realize now, in my case, that it was probably like using a cannon to kill a flea. But I was immensely grateful both to Dr. Ehrlich and to Zdiszek

There again was the advantage of being an "old number" and knowing people. For by this time, probably around February 1944, I had survived in the camp for over a year. I found a Slovak girl I had met in the *Schreibstube* who was a nurse and who would give me the Neosalvarsan shots. I remember they came in the form of two ampules for each shot, one with a powder the other with a liquid. They had to be mixed in the hypodermic and than injected intravenously. I was lucky that the girl was a real nurse who knew how to give intravenous shots. I don't know if it was the Neosalvarsan or the subsiding of the clap by itself, but by March 1944 I was discharged from the hospital as cured and put into the line for work assignment.

Here again, though Freud says there are no coincidences, luck or coincidence, call it what you will, was with me. The *Arbeitsdienstführer,* the one whom I had so foolhardily approached on my first day in Birkenau, was assigning the prisoners to jobs. As I came in front of him, he smiled and said," Ah, the office worker; how about you working in *Kanada* for a while?" And that is where I went, to *Kanada,* the most desirable work detail in all of Birkenau. *Kanada* had received its name because everyone, including the workers there, believed that it was the land of everything: of food, and clothing, and medicine, and anything else our heart desired that came in the transports.

    Kanada was the elite work detail of the women's camp as well as the men's camp. It was the place where everything was available if we were careful enough not to get caught smuggling "organized" items into the camp. The women of *Kanada* did not have to wear the camp-issued underwear, they had access to all the silk and cotton panties they wanted; and they had also bras, an item that was not standard issue in the camp.[2] Handkerchiefs, nightgowns, toothbrushes, nail files, knives, forks, spoons, were all in overabundance in *Kanada.* The *Kanada* work detail collected all the suitcases containing clothing and non-perishable food the victims brought, thinking they were going to a labor camp. They were actually, but only those selected from the doomed that looked useful for a short while.

Upon arrival, the victims were, of course, immediately relieved of all their belongings: suitcases, satchels, knapsacks, all thrown helter-skelter onto the ramp as they descended from the cattle cars where the men from *Kanada* collected everything and brought it to the compound which consisted of a number of warehouses for the specific clothing items, such

---

[2] Brassieres were officially forbidden. Camp underwear was blue and white striped, and very scratchy....If one were caught with underwear "organized" from *Kanada,* one could get punished....Strangely enough the Jewish prisoners were not checked for regulation underwear, only the political prisoners. Unpublished ms. Zippi Tichauer, October 1991.

as men's suits, women's suit, women's dresses, children's clothing, furs, shoes, and other items.

After having been assigned to the *Kanada* work detail, I was, of course, also housed in the *Kanada* sleeping block. It was one of the stone blocks with the oh-so-familiar *"Kojen."* But for the *Kanada* workers the *"Kojen"* served two women as sleeping quarters, not the six or seven that had to make do with one *"Koje"* in the new arrival block. There were straw sacks in the *Kanada* block, and, unbelievably, I remember sheets in those bunks! I suppose, like everything else, they too were smuggled in by the detail, every day, piece by piece, under their clothing, wrapped around them. Since there were no such things as double or queen size sheets, all they had to smuggle in were singles.

Like all newcomers to a day-and-night-shift work detail like *Kanada,* I was assigned to the nightshift. We would march out of the camp to the *Kanada* barracks compound after evening roll call and march back in time for the morning roll call. This work schedule gives you an idea of the workload of the detail. In April 1944, transports were arriving from the West as well as the East. There might have been some, not very many, prisoners transferred from the extermination camps, like Maidanek, Sobibor, Belzec, that had been evacuated ahead of the Russian advance. But the largest numbers of transports during the summer were from Hungary.[3] As the Russians advanced in the East and the Allies began liberating Europe from the West the Nazis were determined to hold and kill as many Jews as possible before the enemy might liberate them.[4] Most of the extermination camps, such as Maidanek, Sobibor and

---

[3] It was not until April 29, 1944, that Hungarian Jews, who had been, until then, under the "protection" of the Hungarian dictator, Admiral Miklos Horthy, began to be deported to Auschwitz after the Germans invaded Hungary and replaced Horthy with a collaborator, Dome Szothjay. Between April and July, 1944, over 437,000 Hungarian Jews were transported to the death camps and concentration camps, victims from the last major country to which the "Final Solution" was applied.

[4] On June 22, 1944 "Operaton Bagration" was launched by the Soviet Army and six weeks later it had routed the German forces on the Eastern front and was at the gates of Warsaw. Most of the concentration and death camps under the Nazis were liberated by the Red Army.

Chelmno were dissolved by the Nazis by killing the inmates or transferring some to Auschwitz, ahead of the Russians, but all that is post-War information, since the Germans, being aware that they had lost the War, were determined not to "lose" the Final Solution. One of the most famous victims of this murderous obsession was poor Anne Frank who arrived in Auschwitz just days before the liberation of Amsterdam.

Of course the transports came with all their luggage and the *Kanada* work detail had to sort, process and expedite into the Reich anything that could be useful. Working in *Kanada* meant that we had everything available to us, but we could not afford to think about where the things that we sorted and bundled for shipment into the Reich came from. We could not afford to put a face to that child's dress, or that woman's skirt, or that man's suit that we bundled ready for shipment. Twenty to a bundle for underwear, ten for children's dresses, three for men's suits, and so forth. No one in the work detail gave it a thought The people in *Kanada* were all "old" prisoners according to Birkenau standards: they had survived, some of them since 1942. They had gone through the worst of the times of the camp: daily selections, typhus, hunger, cold. They had clawed their way up to that work detail mostly through knowing someone who knew someone who had some pull in the work detail, or in the labor allocation office and could get them in. They were people who had lost touch with the normal values of the world outside of Nazi control. They lived for themselves, for their friends, for their group.

The outside world and the deportees that came from that world into theirs had little meaning for the "old" prisoners. That was the reason why little thought was given to the origin of the things they handled, sorted and shipped out. However, some things stuck in your mind, like the one day in June, while I was still working on the sorting heaps, I came across a photo of two young people obviously very much in love. I took a closer look, because something seemed familiar about those two faces. It hit me suddenly: the two young people were Hanni Schleissner and Harry Nelan, two of my group of the *"Haselbacher"* in Prague about a year before the deportations began.

For a minute I just stood with the photo in my hand, as if I were paralyzed. But then I realized that that photo could not be from a recent transport because there had been no transports from Theresienstadt since May of 1944, so there was not much of a chance that either one of them would be alive. I did not keep the photo, what for?

Chapter Ten

1944-1945: *Kanada* and the Death March

Of course one of the greatest advantages in working in *Kanada* was a sort of tacit agreement between the SS-men who guarded the work detail and the prisoners. The SS were strictly forbidden to take anything for themselves from the warehouses. Strangely enough that was considered stealing from the Reich, and was severely punished, even resulting in the offender being sent to the front as the result of being caught.[1]

---

[1] In <u>Joel Brand, die Geschichte eines Geschaefts</u>. ("The Story of a Business") by Heino Kipphard, is a scene in which one of Eichmann's men, reporting on the liquidation of 4500 Jewish apartments, asks him to reconsider the sentence imposed upon an underling for stealing linoleum from an apartment. Eichmann refuses leniency, saying: "Whether eight or eight thousand square. meters, I demand of my people that they are financially clean, above reproach." Susan E. Cernyak-Spatz. <u>German Holocaust Literature</u> .New York: Peter Lang, 1989, p. 74

Even if a prisoner denounced an SS man for stealing, the SS man would be punished. The prisoner might go to the gas or the punishment detail but the rule existed. I do not know how the arrangement evolved, but when I arrived in *Kanada* in March, 1944, it was understood that the prisoners did not "rat" if an SS man stole from a warehouse, and the SS men in charge of the detail left abundance of food that came in the suitcases to the prisoners. There was hard salami, bread, cookies, tins of chicken fat; anything that could be packaged that wouldn't spoil for a long time such as flour, sugar and butter mixed to make a sort of meal that was very nourishing, or canned condensed milk. All that was left for us was pretty evenly divided among all of us who worked in *Kanada*.

There were always people, like the girlfriends of the men who emptied the suitcases, who got the best of everything. But everyone in the work detail eventually got some civilian food. There was always plenty of bread I recall. Bread could have also come from the sales of some of the items that were smuggled into the camp. This, of course, was the bread that the *blockovas* skimmed off the rations in the new arrival blocks. The daily rations would be delivered in bulk to the individual blocks and would then be divided by the *blockovas*. In the new arrival blocks the amount skimmed off by the block personnel was always bigger, because the "stupid" newcomers did not know how much they were supposed to get. In the regular work detail blocks they would not dare do that.

It would seem that the Jewish prisoners, who did not receive the generous packages that the gentile prisoners received, as soon as they were in a position to do so, would barter for anything. If some worked in the agriculture department, they might barter potatoes; the nurses in the hospital block could barter for medications, the kind that they had more of than they needed for their friends. They did not much care whether these medications were badly needed by the sick prisoners as long as these sick prisoners were not someone they knew, or an old prisoner, who had some pull[2]. It was the newcomers who got the short end of everything.

Smuggling items for our fellow prisoners from *Kanada* was a rather tricky thing, as long as we were housed in Birkenau and marched to the *Kanada* barracks, which were on the way to the main camp. We put on two layers of pants, and bras, sweaters, or blouses, whatever was manageable. If there was frisking at the gate, we were usually forewarned, because the *Kanada* work detail was, as a rule, the last work detail to march in. If such a message was passed down the line, the area around the work detail would be littered in no time with all kinds of clothing because so long as the SS did not find anything directly on us, they did not care to pursue the matter any further. They just collected the items for themselves. It did seem strange that there was rarely if ever any punishment meted out for

---

[2] Zippi Tichauer reports that she would have the *Kanada* women bring her any cod-liver oil, for vitamin subsidy and prontosil, a bladder infection medication which often could be found in the suitcases, since she knew the value of these medications for maintaining their health. Unpublished ms . Zippi Tichauer, October 1991.

smuggling. Perhaps, since they never found anything on a particular prisoner, and they could not punish the entire work detail as it was too valuable as trained processors of a source of income for the Nazis, they probably looked for bigger fish to fry at that time. Things did begin to look to the Nazis by now as if their defeat would be inevitable.

My first night on the nightshift was rather eventful. I don't remember how it came about, but we were working side by side with the men, sorting the heaps of clothes that had come in from a new transport. We would separate the different articles of clothing that then would be carried to the different barracks to be bundled into neat packages to be shipped to the Reich. I had started talking with a German-Jewish boy named Ralph when suddenly he bluntly asked me: "Are you not the one who just came from the hospital after a bout with VD?" I could have sunk into the ground. But I quickly made up a story about a mistake having been made in the lab, and that it was not my test that had come back positive. That was why I was let out from the hospital and came to *Kanada.* To this day I don't know how the story got around so fast. But I guess by that time among the old prisoners there were not too many secrets. After all, there were not so many of us left in 1944.

The *Kanada* work detail had a different atmosphere from any other, or even the *Schreibstube,* which was pretty elite. Here everyone cared for everyone else, we stuck together, and even the newcomer was somehow protected. Since this was a work detail that was not threatened or jockeying for positions or favoritism from the *Kapo,* the groups that formed among the women in *Kanada* were not mainly for support and sustenance as in new arrival barracks, or even inside details, like the *Schreibstube,* where competition was always keen, but they were formed for friendship and companionship. The only people from the camp that I am still in touch with today are the ones still alive from the *Kanada* detail.

That first night in *Kanada* my theatrical abilities came in handy once more. About two or three in the morning the whole work detail would bunk down on the clothing heaps inside the barracks and go to sleep until it was time to march back into the camp. One SS-officer was eying me during the evening, walking by and looking me over. When all was quiet in the barracks, I felt a gentle kick on my foot. I sort of opened one eye and saw the young officer standing at the foot of the heap, motioning me to follow him outside. Well, I was not about to submit to another rape, what it would have been, certainly not anything by consent. So I pretended to be deeply enough asleep not to notice the uniform and kick of the boot. The two boots were the closest thing in my line of vision and I had to make it look like I did not know what I was doing to an SS-man. He disappeared not wanting to make a scene in the barracks: embarrassing for him; fatal for me.

Yes, there were some sexual relations between Jewish prisoners and SS-men.

Discovery would end with the SS-man being sent to the front and the prisoner to the gas except for Hindu Citron, among the very first transports from Slovakia. She was a beautiful, innocent-looking girl, with big brown eyes, and a round face, like a healthy country girl. She must have attracted many an SS-man. Her good looks, even in Russian uniforms, must have been her salvation, for she was one of the oldest members of the *Kanada* detail, which had been formed right in the beginning of the establishment of Birkenau, around September or October 1942. She and SS-*Rottenführer* (corporal) Franz Wunsch must have met shortly after her arrival in the camp.[3] Looking back at

---

[3] Franz Wunsch, a virulent Jew-hater, fell in love with Hindu (Helene) Citron when he was the chief of the first *Kanada* Department in Birkenau. Hindu was sick with typhus, and he helped her hide in the *Effektenkammer* (clothing department) because she was afraid in the Jewish hospital block she would be taken in one of the daily selections there. He visited her every day while she was sick there, and according to his post-War testimony fell in love with her there, and was a changed person from that time on. He would not work in selections and did not beat any women any more as he had been known to do before. Hermann Langbein, Menschen in Auschwitz, Frankfurt: Verlag Ullstein, GmbH, 1972, pp.459-460.

that period of time, I am convinced that anyone who survived Birkenau for more than six months had a job either in administration or a work detail that did not do outside work. Outside work details were designed for speedy descent into *Muselmann* status, and the crematorium. I do not know whether the same system of mutual support worked in the men's camp among those who had survived the first few weeks and were able to get out of the outside work detail. There must have been something similar among them. A Jew did not become an "old" prisoner by working long on the outside detail.

People in *Kanada* were alternating from nightshift to dayshift in rotation. When I was on the day shift, I did the same thing as on the night shift, sorting the clothes from the transports.

But the problems of being a prisoner would stay with me even when I thought I was in a secure position as is illustrated by the following incident in which my vulnerability to the whims of the Nazi administrators could alter my fate in one way or another

One day as I was carrying a large bundle of some clothing to one of the barracks, the *Arbeitsdienstführer*, who had originally assigned me to *Kanada,* was walking through the yard and saw me. He grabbed me, got someone to take my bundle, and took me to the SS-man in charge of the warehouse. He told the warehouse chief "I assigned this prisoner to work in the office since she is an office worker. Find a place for her." The warehouse chief had to comply since he was the lower-ranking officer. The regular secretary, Alice, happened to be out for the day with a cold or something. In *Kanada* we could afford to stay in the block to recuperate from an illness without being sent to Block 25 and the gas. When she came back, we both worked in the office.

The work was not very complicated. It was just bookkeeping, keeping a record of how many bundles were brought in from the sorting barracks, and how many bundles of each item were shipped to the Reich. I assume that the freight cars used to ship the clothing to the Reich were the same that had brought a transport the previous day. After having been cleaned they were used to bring the products of the "Death Factory" back to the Fatherland; a typical example of German efficiency. The members of the warehouse crew were the elite of the Slovakian survivors: Hindu Citron, Tischa and Cilka, two sisters. Tischa was in the warehouse with us, and Cilka the younger of the two, was the personal servant of the head of the department. Then there was little Alice, big Alice with me in the office, Olga the Greek, the only non-Slovak except me, Katja Grünberger and, big Manci who, as far as I know, was the only Jewish woman *Kapo*. All of the above named women, with the exception of Manci, whose fate I do not know, live today in Israel, all quite successful, most of them widowed. Men just are not as sturdy as women.

There were also several male workers in the warehouse, all of them furriers, who also helped stacking the bundles. There was Maurice Schellevies (Schellekes) the Dutchman, Adi from

Brussels, and Norman Loper from Vienna. They were all old prisoners who had gotten the jobs when there was a demand in *Kanada* for furriers. Maybe they were not all furriers, but Maurice had been a furrier in Holland and he quickly taught the other men how to take furs apart and remove the fur linings from men's and women's coats. In short, thanks to Maurice they all worked in the warm barracks, and were safe, whether they were really skilled or not.

The three of them used to cut up furs, claiming they were unusable to be shipped out, and would make insoles and warm fur vests for many men and women prisoners to wear under their clothing. Of course the recipients of these gifts would have to be on inside work assignments, because outside workers were constantly frisked and would never have been able to hide any fur vests or insoles. Maurice wrote his story after the war for a deposition in a war crime trial. He refused to go to Germany as requested, but sent the notarized manuscript. I use his testimony in my Holocaust course to this day. He was very gratified that his story was used to inform the next generations about the Holocaust

One day in May, 1944 before we were transferred to Birkenau, to the *Brzezinki Effekten Lager*, there was an air raid on the camp area. As soon as the alarm sounded, the SS men disappeared, God knows where they had a shelter, but the *Kanada* compound was deserted by them. With each bomb that we heard exploding we cheered. I will never forget Maurice and I stood at one of the high windows in the prefab building that was the warehouse. I remember we climbed on a stack of bundles; I don't remember what they were, but we were determined to reach the window, which was open. There we stood singing at the top of our voices: "We're hanging our washing on the Siegfried line, if the Siegfried line's still there." That was one of the British Army songs. Many years later, when I mentioned this incident during an interview on TV in Charlotte, NC, I received a phone call from a very nice lady, who had a record with that song on it. I think that must have been the first time that we felt that perhaps the world had not totally forgotten us, that they knew we were there.

Unfortunately, it seems one of the bombs hit a block in Auschwitz I and killed some prisoners. The bombings were carried out by the Russians; the Allies never tried to bomb Auschwitz for "strategic reasons."[4] I wonder if at that point we cared if a bomb would fall into the *Kanada* compound; we just wanted to see results and prayed for more raids. It was an incredible high. Of course there were still more than eight months to go before we left Birkenau, and many brave prisoners lost their lives at that horrible ending, but that day in May we felt that for the first time there might be life and not just

---

[4] There was an American air raid on the IG Farben slave labor camp (Buna) on December 6, 1944. On January 14, 1945 an American reconnaissance plane flew over the area to check for damage taking very precise photos of Birkenau. Martin Gilbert, Auschwitz and the Allies, New York: Holt, Rinehart and Winston, 1981, cited in Czech, pp. 950, 961.However, the Allies never bombed the railway lines to prevent the transportation of Jews to Auschwitz.

the crematorium waiting for us, as we had continually been told. Sometime during the beginning of June, I don't recall the exact date, the *Kanada* work detail was transferred to a separate camp, meaning the men and the women of the work detail would be housed in a separate small camp to reduce the smuggling or, perhaps, since the Brzezinki camp was located right behind the big Sauna next to Cremo 4 and 5, it was more convenient to have the trains that brought the transport right there ready to be loaded with the sorted clothing and goods from *Kanada.* Why it was called Brzezinki, God knows, since that is simply the Polish form of Birkenau.

The Brzezinki camp consisted of two women's sleeping barracks and I think three men's, and a number of large pre-fabs housing the victims' and prisoners' property. The fence around the camp was not electrified since the camp was within the perimeter of the large electric fence surrounding Birkenau. In Brzezinki the members of the detail had the luxurious privilege of a shower every night in the big Sauna with as much hot water as one wanted. Of course we did our best to sabotage the Reich by using and discarding as much clothes and sheets and blankets as we could.

In summer the women would wear slacks and men's shirts, which we ironed as well as possible. We had one ironing board in the main warehouse which was the barrack where the bundled clothes would be collected to be loaded on the train to the Reich. That is also where my office was, or better the office of the chief of the warehouse whose secretary I was. His name was Armbruster and he was an older man, about 50, a former accountant.

The women of the warehouse were, of course, "my group"; we were about 20. The dress uniform for the winter was ski pants, men's shirts, and crewneck, or v-neck sweaters with the collar of the shirt outside. This, of course, meant you only had to iron the collar and cuffs in winter. The sheets on the beds--bunk beds, two-tiered, with straw sacks--would be used maybe one or two nights, then duly ripped into strips and dumped into the latrine. That was as much sabotaging as we could do.

One other event buoyed my spirits, and I really don't know how many people in the camp were aware of it. It must have been around June 6th. I had stayed in the camp, as I had an appointment with the dentist. Dentist appointments usually meant a tooth to pull. That is the way I lost all my back teeth. That day I had an appointment for one more to be pulled. Another advantage of being an old prisoner was that I did not have to worry about walking around in the deserted camp and being asked questions by a *Kapo* or an SS-man or matron what I was doing there. I had my permission slip to stay in camp and visit the dentist.

It must have been around noon and the camp was absolutely deserted, except for a few people: *blockovas*, runners, matrons, on the camp street. All of a sudden *Lagersperre* (curfew) was announced over a loudspeaker. That meant everyone had better hurry into a building and stay there until the curfew was lifted. I ran to the dental station in the hospital compound. I don't remember who was there, near a radio, or if it was perhaps the SS-dentist who told his prisoner assistant what he had heard, but I was told that the curfew had been called because that day the Allies had landed in Normandy. I guess they were afraid there could be a joyous riot.

But strangely enough, nothing happened. Curfew was lifted, life went on, but there was an undertone of excitement. For most of us, that had been the only information we had received about the War since we had entered the camp. We had known about Stalingrad before I came to Birkenau, but that had been the last war news I had gotten. At least we could hope now that there might be an end to the War in sight. This gave us all the more reason not to make waves so our survival could be assured. I realize it sounds strange, but none of us average prisoners knew about the War in the Pacific. I am sure that some privileged prisoners every so often heard some radio news and were better informed, but for us the information about the Pacific theatre was unexpected news.

I suppose it was beginning with my *Aussenkommando* experience, after the hours and hours of roll calls, after my return from the *Stabsgebäude*, after the daily selections, the typhus, the starvation, that led to the onset of my doubts about the existence of a God. People experienced miracles of survival they ascribed to God's intervention. Perhaps my miracle should have been the time that I described in chapter five, in Birkenau, when I thought that the earth was swallowing me up, and I resisted with all my might, and stayed alive. But even that moment did not make me think of a God.

How could anyone think of a loving God who watches over everyone of us, when that God would have looked down on Birkenau and its smoking chimneys? How could anyone, even the most fanatically religious Jewish believer, contemplate that the kind of suffering delivered unto us could have anything to do with the will of an almighty God? That in itself would be almost blasphemous. I laugh at any survivors who claim that the suffering they endured strengthened their faith. I despise such hypocrisy. I would hope that Saul Friedländer, the eminent Holocaust historian, was right in his assertion of God having averted his face from mankind during the Holocaust.[5] Maybe God is back now, though is he? I feel so incredibly disdainful of the claims of those who believe in the divine intervention in human lives.

On whose side is the one God ? On the monotheistic Jewish side, on the monotheistic Muslim side, on the monotheistic Christian side? Perhaps the Greek or Roman concept of the gods with human foibles was simpler; it did not demand unquestioning adherence. I cannot believe in the God that should have saved ME and let millions die, and what did they die for: their faith? No, they died due to hatred and fanatic bigotry and to satisfy the greed and the

---

[5] Saul Friedländer. The Jews in European History. Cincinnati: Hebrew Union College, 1994.

lowest instincts of an entire "so-called civilized" nation. Raul Hilberg was right when he said that Hitler took to the extreme the anti-Semitic development of Jewish persecution since the beginning of anti-Semitism in the modern era.[6]

The bombing raids never amounted to much. I suppose the mission was not important enough to actually hit and destroy the crematoriums. Not that the Allies did not know where they were. After the war plenty of aerial photography was displayed showing the exact locations of the crematoria. Supposedly humanitarian considerations kept the Allies from bombing the Cremos. Whose lives did they consider? Ours were forfeited anyway. Strange decisions were made in that situation. It would seem that either the British or the Americans

---

[6] Since the fourth century there have been three anti-Jewish policies: conversion, expulsion and annihilation. The second appeared as an alternative to the first, and the third appeared as an alternative to the second....Three stages of persecution: 1.Drive the Jews into Christianity (conversion) 2.Drive the Jews into exile (expulsion) 3. Drive the Jews into their death (annihilation). Nazis did not begin the development, they completed it. Raul Hilberg. The Destruction of the European Jews, Chicago: Quadrangle Books, introduction, p.3 ff.

decided that bombing Auschwitz and Birkenau, mainly the crematoria, could endanger the lives of the prisoners. So it was left to the Russians to do the few raids on Auschwitz. By this time the Allies were well informed of the murder machine in Poland, and that the prisoners' lives at that point in time were forfeited anyway. The survivors cannot help but think that it must have been one of the century-old reactions of most European countries: It's just Jews, why bother?

Shortly after that raid, the work detail was transferred to Brzezinki. We were not all selected to go to Brzezinki with the detail. Those of us who were chosen to go considered themselves very lucky. There was no better work detail than *Kanada*. The men and women who were dismissed had to get used to living a much-diminished life as far as non-prisoner food and non-prison clothing was concerned. They probably all found jobs inside the camp because most of them were low-number prisoners and therefore were given certain considerations by the prisoner-administrated job allocations department.

Those of us going to the new camp, located behind the new Sauna, between Cremos 3 and 4, were housed there in two sleeping barracks for the women, at the entrance to the camp, in front of the gate that closed the warehouse area. The men's barracks were at the opposite end of the camp. There were 25 standard prefab barracks used as storage sheds for the different sorts of clothing, one one-story pre-fab as the main warehouse for the finished bundles of merchandise, and one one-story pre-fab housing and office for the chief of the department, SS-*Hauptscharführer* Werner Hahn.

In this period from mid-summer to the end of 1944, the group in Brzezinki probably was and felt least threatened of all the work details. At that time there was no longer any civilian clothing available in the Reich, and the officers and personnel of the Auschwitz compound probably supplied many families and relatives with clothing and valuables, stolen from

Brzezinki. All the suitcases collected from the Hungarian transports that arrived at the rate of two or three per day, all the clothing from the Cremos, and from those selected to enter the camp were to be sorted, bundled and sent into the Reich, to be distributed by the government to, I presume, victims of Allied bombing raids and displaced persons.

By that time the Germans were losing more and more territory and there were many German refugees who needed to be supplied. But despite that, and though it was strictly forbidden, the personnel of Auschwitz-Birkenau used Brzezinki as their department store. After all, the clothing was not counted until it was bundled and in the warehouse. What disappeared out of the barracks, be it coats, dresses, shoes, or other materials, were unaccounted for.

The prisoners in *Kanada* had one perfect way to sabotage the efforts of the Third Reich. We, especially in Brzezinki, took all the clothes we could use to wear, each day, and destroyed them and threw them into the latrines that night. If we count about 500 people doing that day by day, it amounted to a tidy loss of clothing. Not much, but after all, we felt we did something, and we were safe. There were no selections in Brzezinki.

In the fall of 1944, when the Hungarian transports seemed to have exhausted their supply of victims, a new source of fodder for the Cremos was found: the parents of the first Jewish prisoners in Auschwitz, the Slovakian girls who had been coerced to "volunteer" for pioneer labor camps with the promise that their parents and family would be protected from any deportation. In the Fall of 1944, that promise, like most promises of the Third Reich given to Jews such as the protection of World War I veterans from deportation, was broken. In one of those transports was Hindu Citron's sister with her children. Hindu managed to save her with the help of *Rottenführer* Wunsch but could not save the children.

As the year 1944 came to an end, we heard more and more rumors about the War going very badly for the Germans. A revolt in Cremo IV on October 8, 1944 brought the gassing almost to a stop. The members of the *Sonderkommando*, those whose responsibility it was to take the corpses from the gas chambers to be incinerated, killed three Nazi guards and blew up one of the crematoria. Several hundred managed to escape although most were captured and four women, the most notable, the heroic Rosa Robota, were hanged before the entire camp. The last gassing occurred on Nov.2, 1944; from that time on, according to Danuta Czech, selected prisoners were shot.[7] From the *Kanada* work detail more and more men were sent "on transport." We only knew that they were sent into the Reich.

In the Fall of 1944, I had a strange and interesting experience. In chapter six I had mentioned the young SS-man who interviewed

---

[7] Czech, p.934 f.

me in the *Stabsgebäude* on my transfer there in February 1943. He was the one who had an American father and a German mother, Perry Broad. One cannot have a more average American name. But Perry was an SS-man; however, one with strange tastes, like American jazz, English books, and so forth. When I met him again, I remember it must have been not too late into the season, because there was no snow yet. I was called one early afternoon to the office of the "old man," the head of the detail, SS-*Hauptscharführer* Werner Hahn. I quickly tried to think if there was anything I had done wrong, perhaps an addition or subtraction mistake in the invoices that went with the collected clothing into the Reich, but I could not think of anything.

With some trepidation I went to the office, and there sat Perry Broad, drinking coffee with Hahn, in friendly conversation. He greeted me very cordially, but of course no handshake, and Hahn said: "Perry wants you to go to the *Politische Abteilung* with him for a little music." It seems Broad had remembered that I was also a jazz lover and I must have mentioned that I had done some jazz singing in Theresienstadt. A young Dutch prisoner had also been called to the office. How Broad knew that he was a musician also, I do not know. Anyway, he had come by bicycle from the *Politische*, which was in the men's camp behind Brzezinki, and so the three of us started out, Broad pushing his bike, and the Dutch man and I walking along.

The situation at that time was already so relaxed among old prisoners that there were no normal camp rules being obeyed, such as walking at least one meter distance from any SS personnel or not talking unless spoken to. I don't know what this "mixed breed" German was thinking, but it surely had little to do with camp rules. We spent the afternoon singing, accompanied by Broad on an accordion, which he played very well. Other SS men from the *Politische Abteilung* came by and looked in on us, but nothing was said, and there were no complaints about this kind of fraternization.

Broad took us back to Brzezinki so we would be in time for roll call and that was that. It was like a moment out of time, three young people making music without any regard to the deep gulf of enmity that separated them.

During December of 1944 the mood change in the SS was almost visible, at least among our SS personnel. Mr. Armbruster, the chief of the warehouse, my boss, brought me more and more cookies from his wife's baking, and cigarettes, and he would stay after the so-called office hours were over more often at 7 p.m. and talk.

One night, over cigarettes, I took my courage in my hands and decided to ask him a question I had wanted to ask for a long time. Armbruster had been a guard on the *Weisskäppchen* detail, the rag-picking detail I had been in for one of my outside detail jobs. And he had been as cruel and indifferent to any suffering he saw there as were all the other guards. So, that is the question I put to him that evening in the quiet office in Brzezinki.

He looked at me for a minute, and then he said: "You know Susie, that is easy to explain. Here you sit with me, as a well-spoken well-groomed young woman, though a prisoner, but I know you as a human being, as a person. Those women in the *Weisskäppchen* detail were not human beings, they did not look like human beings, like women. They were stinking skeletons, things that one hated to be around, that one just as soon beat off.

"I sometimes wonder whether that was not done on purpose, so we of the SS would not mind beating or killing those things, because after all, I know for myself, I am an older man than most of these men, and I should have had some compassion, but I did not."

Many times when I show the film, "The Wannsee Conference" in my Holocaust history classes, I have to think that among the decisions made at that conference, one of them must have been another rationale for dehumanizing the prisoners to the extent that it was done. That kind of sadistic approach made it so much easier for the SS and the matrons to be ruthless and cruel.

On the night from January 17 to 18, 1945 the entire Auschwitz complex, Auschwitz I, II and III, was evacuated into the Reich. And with that order began the "Death March."

That night the chief of the *Kanada* work detail, Werner Hahn, came into the women's and men's sleeping barracks and advised all of us to go immediately into the warehouse barracks and supply ourselves with as much warm clothing as we could find, take knapsacks, and stuff them with socks and underwear and other clothing items to keep us warm. As he put it to us, "we are going on a long walk." To this day I am not sure whether the rumors were true about him, that he was a double agent, or whether he simply had an attack of humanity.

It was Hahn and his two acolytes, the Blind One (Weise) and the Lame One, who stuck with us, on the long march through snow-covered forest trails knee-deep in snow. Were we evacuated because the Germans were afraid the Russians might liberate us, or was it simply the fact that they were determined to complete the goal of the Final Solution down to the last Jew, since they had by then accepted the fact that they had lost the War? Be that as it may, the order of the day was, "Bullet in the head who cannot walk." Only recently have I been informed, by Zippi Tichauer, that the Russians were practically in hailing distance, and that the flares we saw going off while walking in the woods right after leaving the camp were Russian flares. It seems the Russian strategy did not include liberating Auschwitz-Birkenau with the full complement of SS and prisoners in it. The Russians bypassed the camp, and when the marching prisoners were long gone, on January 27, to be precise, the Russians sent a detachment with a first-class camera crew back to "liberate" the 9000 sick people who had remained behind.

On the march of at least two days and two nights, as I seem to recall, the roads of the forest were lined with bodies. Quite a few girls in the *Kanada* group of approximately 300 women disappeared into the woods as soon as they had the opportunity. Most of them were Polish girls who spoke the language fluently and obviously trusted their compatriots more than I would. Our group from the warehouse of *Kanada*, 15 of us, stuck together and did not go "over the hill." Were we cowards, or did we simply feel secure under the protection of our three SS-men who stuck with us?

We finally came to a small railroad junction called Löslau. There a long line of freight cars, open and closed ones, were waiting for us. How important the completion of the Final Solution was to the Germans was obvious from the fact that at the point when they needed every warm body and every means of transportation to defend the Fatherland, they did not mind using hundreds of personnel and freight cars to deport the 58,000 or so prisoners from Auschwitz into the Reich.

As we were herded towards the train, Hahn directed us to an open coal car. We protested, but he insisted that with enough people in the car, and some of the straw that we found at the station, we had a better chance of survival than in the closed car. And he was so right! Upon our arrival in Ravensbrück, when the sealed closed freight cars were opened, many a body tumbled out. We might have been cold, but we had air, and at any stop, although we were given no food, we could hop out and drink snow, eat snow, wash with snow: we survived.

The train wound its way slowly towards the Reich. It stopped and started numerous times, due, I presume, to troop trains or other military priorities. The train moved through a big city, and Hahn, who was in the open coal freight car with us, said: " Look at Berlin!" What a satisfying sight that was for us who so suffered under the Reich! Bombed out, destroyed, dilapidated, the great city of Berlin, a city I had loved, but that now gave me great "Schadenfreude"—pleasure in another's misery-- to see what it had sunk to. That night, probably a day and a night after our departure from Löslau, we arrived in Ravensbrück, the only women's concentration camp in the Reich. Strangely enough Ravensbrück, that notorious women's camp, was located close to a lake where my cousin Hannelore and I, on Sunday outings with our parents, got our first swimming lesson, paddling in a spare tire tube, held by Uncle Siegfried's chauffeur, Herr Lisser. That must have been in 1934 or so. Now this lovely landscape was marred by the biggest concentration camp compound for women in the Reich. It was neighboring to the man's camp, Sachsenhausen, also located north of Berlin.

Chapter Eleven
Winter-Spring 1945- Liberation!

We arrived in Ravensbrück sometime in the middle of the night. It must have been several days after January 18, the night we left Birkenau. There were many other Birkenau women in the coal car with us, and they, too, had been saved by Hahn's insistence. We 15 remaining from *Kanada* made sure we stayed together. They marched us to the *"Jugendlager."* The barracks that they put us in were totally empty, no bunks, no water, nothing. The snow was deep outside; it seemed to reach the windowsills of the barracks. At least the windows could be opened, and we could gather some of the snow, again, for drinking, eating, and crawling out of the windows to relieve ourselves.

There was one moment there that is deeply etched in my memory: One of the matrons whom we knew to be absolutely inhuman from our Birkenau experience came into the barracks of highly agitated women, crammed into a space meant for probably half our number. We all clamored for water, for food, for a place to sit or lie down. I think at that point all of us must have had the feeling that there was a chance of survival, that the War might end before they would finish us.

There was bravado in us as we tried to assert ourselves as human beings to our tormentors. And the matron's response was: "You Jewish whores, be grateful that you are still alive: you really have no right to live anymore anyway." How it must have galled these beasts in women's clothing, when not three months later they distributed Red Cross packages to the "Jewish whores" as the first recipients, under the watchful eyes of the Red Cross bus drivers. I'm not sure she was with the matrons when the Red Cross packages were given out. She just was one of that ilk. But

I can recall the sound of that raucous voice when she uttered her vicious words.

From some of the other women prisoners, the few that came near the crowded barracks in the *Jugendlager*, the so-called "youth camp" where the gas chamber had been built, we heard some rumors about its existence in Ravensbrück. But somehow we did not pay any attention to these rumors; we had survived Birkenau; the Third Reich was not going to get us now. However, it seems not to have been built exclusively for the Final Solution like the Birkenau gas chambers. Ravensbrück, until the survivors of the Death March were brought into it, had disposed of all its Jewish prisoners long before that.

The day came, some days after our arrival, that all the women from Birkenau were assembled on what must have been the *Appellplatz* (parade ground) and word got around that it was to be a selection of where the women would be sent to: the various sub camps of Ravensbrück. Like all large concentration camps, Ravensbrück had a number of sub camps which usually were small compounds near a factory or mine that exploited the prisoners from the main camp. We 15 who had started out from Brzezinki with 25 from the warehouse, while some of the Polish girls had disappeared on the Death March stood together again. And again our three Brzezinki SS-men, Hahn, Weise, and the Lame One, must have asserted I don't know what kind of authority to succeed in pulling us 15 out of the selections. As we found out through rumors, they had maintained that we were experts in the warehousing of the prisoners' clothing-- *Effektenspezialisten*--and that our expertise was urgently needed in a place like Ravensbrück. I still wonder how they got away with it because Ravensbrück was a much older installation than Birkenau, with probably plenty of experience in warehousing prisoner clothing. It had a clothing warehouse where all the clothing of the political prisoners was catalogued and kept for their eventual release so they did not really need our "expert advice." Be that as it may, we were registered into Ravensbrück and assigned to a block.

There the prisoner housing was luxurious compared to what had been provided in Birkenau for the main women's camp. Here each of the women had a bed--I can't recall whether they were two level bunk beds or single beds-- and they had sheets, blue and white checked, and pillowcases, and blankets. This would have been unheard of in the "normal" blocks in Birkenau.

The morning after the selection (which was at least not a selection for the gas chamber) we assembled at the gate after roll call and formed our three rows of five. The old man and his subordinates came to get us, checked us out from the *Blockführer,* and marched us to a prefab barrack about 10 or 15 minutes from the main camp. Inside that barrack was an office space on the right side, the rest being an open area with a bathroom at the back. Ravensbrück had normal plumbing, unlike Birkenau's latrines.

We found heaps of mostly rags, and clothing that looked like it had been shipped from Brzezinki, so we would have something to do. Outside of the barracks ran a rail line where they shipped in supplies for the camp.

We would keep our eyes open for some food items, like potatoes, that might be brought in in the freight cars. If there was one such shipment, we would wait until the prisoners unloading the car would go to lunch, usually leaving the car door open, and then we would steal potatoes, as much as we could carry in our aprons.

We would cook the potatoes, slice them and bake them on the little potbellied stove in the barracks. They were very filling, and after the hungry days of the march and the time in the *Jugendlager*, anything tasted good. The rations from camp were about the same as in Birkenau, only I remember the bread was much better and the noon soup that was brought out in the ubiquitous kettles on hand-drawn carts by the kitchen detail, was somewhat better as well. But then in Brzezinki we had not eaten the soup very often. Here we were grateful for it, for aside from the potatoes, it was the only warm food we got.

One night, I don't remember how long we had been in Ravensbrück, our work detail was called out in the middle of the night. It must have been the beginning of April, because that was the time when the Red Cross busses started to arrive shortly after. The old man was waiting for us at the gate and we marched through very dark woods. I think it was quite cold still. We at least had our warm clothing from Birkenau. How they knew the way I'll never know, but we arrived at what seemed a substantial brick building, the Ravensbrück *Kleiderkammer*, the place where all the prisoners' clothing was kept. It seemed the old man had a list of how many dresses, shoes, stockings, underwear, and coats he was to bring, in what sizes. Or perhaps, we brought the clothing of certain prisoners. Anyway we had to carry all that back to the camp and handed it over to some matrons. Not until the next day did we find out what it was all about. It seems the Germans had asked the Allies for a prisoner exchange: Allied POWs for German POWs. But since the Allies knew that the POW camps were bearable for the Allied soldiers, they demanded that the Germans give them KZ prisoners in exchange for their soldiers. And the first KZ prisoners they wanted were the women of Ravensbrück. Any political women, or Allied women, whom they might have caught in the underground were of course in Ravensbrück if they had not been executed.

So as not to hand them over in the Ravensbrück prisoner clothing, which would not have looked too good, the Nazis decided to get their civilian clothes and clean them up before the Red Cross came to liberate the prisoners. The rumor was that they put them in the hospital and fed them vitamins and civilian food to make them a bit healthier-looking. I don't know if that was true. But it would have been easy, since they had in Ravensbrück as well as in Birkenau loads of Red Cross packages that had been sent for the prisoners which the Nazis had hoarded for themselves.

A few days later, as we marched into the camp in the afternoon, there were three big white buses with red crosses on them. Upon marching in we, of course, had to stand in roll call. The drivers of the buses had come in while the Red Cross boxes were unloaded. I am sure the SS tried to keep them out, but no luck. They called all the Jewish prisoners out of the roll call to the *Blockführer* hut (administrative hut). There were not very many of us, of course. The majority of the Birkenau prisoners had been sent to the subcamps. Thus we were the very first in line for the distribution of the packages.

The head matron, standing inside the building behind the counter, had opened one of the packages. On top were about five or six packs of cigarettes, and she started to reach for them to take them out to prevent us from having them. But one of the bus drivers stopped her and I can still hear SS-*Untersturmführer* Schwarzhuber, who was standing next to the matron, saying," Let them smoke; what difference does it make? All this here will go up in smoke anyway." I guess in April of 1945 he was not afraid of being denounced or demoted. In fact, on April 30, 1945, the Russian Army arrived to liberate the camp.

The Red Cross buses kept coming and taking out one nationality group after the other: the Austrians, the Czech, the Germans. I probably could have gone with anyone of them, but I was loyal to my group. And before the Slovak's turn came, since most of our group were Slovaks, the Germans, hearing the artillery fire from Berlin, decided it was time to decamp.

During one of the last few weeks, the old man, Hahn, used to call me into his office where he had a radio. He could always say he needed a letter written since I was a secretary in Birkenau, but he didn't even bother with these pretenses. He would say: "Susie come in here and translate the English news, so I know at least what is going on in Hameln" (his hometown). And sure enough, one day the BBC reported that Hameln was occupied.

Again we were journeying on the road. But this time it was in the spring, April, 28, which meant there was no snow or cold. Since the women of Ravensbrück represented a prisoner exchange, the deportation was not as inhuman as the Death March. We were continually told: "Don't stay behind; the Russians will get you and rape you," but there were no shootings that we could see from our place in the column.

We marched at a good clip that first day, and as we stopped at the side of the road for a rest, again herded by our 3 guards--the old man, the Lame One and the Blind One--we wanted to just plunk down on the first green spot near the road. But the old man, for whatever reason, insisted that we go up to the small wood at the edge of the meadow. Reluctantly we dragged ourselves under the first trees of the little wood.

All of a sudden a fighter plane came roaring practically through the wood above our heads and sprayed the meadow of refugees in front of us. To this day I could not tell if it was a Russian, American, or whatever Allied plane. All I know is that once again Werner Hahn, the old man, had saved 15 Jewish girls from possible injury or death.

I know we did a great deal of walking that first day. We were marching west. All the Nazis seemed interested in was getting us to the American lines, actually getting themselves to the American lines. They all knew what would happen to them if the Russians caught up with them. They were all old enough to remember how the German Army had rampaged through Russia and it was clear to them that if they were captured by the Russians, they would be shown no mercy.

I seem to remember that we marched all the way through that first night. I see us on a paved road, with the moon lighting our way as we marched in a ragged formation, the three guards sticking close to us to make sure we 15 were all together.

It is quite possible that during that deportation other women simply stayed behind in some of the villages that we went through. Many of the women in the column were German political prisoners and not afraid of the civilian population which by that time literally smelled the end of the War. Little bits and pieces of memory keep coming back to me from that period. I remember we stayed one night of the trek in the subcamp Malchow, where I saw my friend, Dagmar Ostermann, the girl who had befriended me in the *Stabsgebäude* in 1943. It seems she had been caught writing a letter to her mother and had been sent to the punishment detail. However, being a very old prisoner, and being a political, and only half-Jewish to boot, she was not as badly off in the punishment detail as most of the prisoners there. She was, however, sent on transport probably sometime in November or December and ended up in Ravensbrück thereby saving herself from the Death March. I told her about it and our time in Ravensbrück, and we promised each other to try and keep in touch. We did not manage to do that until sometime during the 60's when we both were married and mothers of children of the same age. I guess most of us survivors had to prove to ourselves quickly that we were not physically damaged and capable of having children.

Another incident of that deportation comes to my mind. We stopped at a country inn by a small bridge over a creek. It seems the bridge was blown up and we had to get over it to go where I suppose the old man knew we had to go. Though the bridge was destroyed, the span was still covered by two beams. The old man had us carry all the tables out of the inn, which was deserted, and we pushed the tables on the beams, until the tables formed a way to cross the creek. The creek ran through a small gulch and some fainthearted women decided to slide down the side of the gulch and wade through the creek, but I and most of my group walked across on the tables. I'd bet if I would be asked to do something like that today, I would say: "No way."

The morning of May 1st, while we marched on a two-lane highway, surrounded by Germans fleeing the Russians, it seemed as if all of the eastern part of Germany was on the road. Suddenly a motorcycle with sidecar, driven by a soldier, roared by, and he yelled as loud as he could "The *Führer* is dead." He had committed suicide the previous day by swallowing cyanide and then shooting himself. Well, it seemed within minutes the long column halted, and out of nowhere schnapps and wine bottles appeared and everybody was congratulating everybody that the War was over although it didn't end officially until May 7 when the Commander-in-Chief of the Army, Alfred Jodl, accepted the terms of surrender from the Allies. We prisoners of Ravensbrück were simply included in the celebration. "We're free now," we shouted. But strangely enough we felt safer with our guards than on our own, and stuck with them marching on.

How they knew where they were going I don't know. I presume they had their roadmaps. At one point we found ourselves on a fairly narrow country lane. All of a sudden there was a commotion ahead of us. The column stopped and a vehicle made its way slowly through the column towards us. It was a squat open vehicle. It had to be an automobile because it had a driver in front, and two men in khaki uniforms in the backseat. Everybody got very excited and afraid because they noticed a large white star on the square hood of the vehicle. "Russian" everyone muttered. We did not know any other star insignia.

But as the strange vehicle approached, I noticed that below the windshield it said "Daisy-Mae." Well I knew that Daisy Mae was not Russian, though of course I had no idea of Little Abner and Co. Since I was the only one in the group who spoke some school English, I approached the vehicle, and asked the driver if he could help us. "Why?" he said. "You speak English!!" I told him that I had learned it in school and would he please liberate us. He looked at me as if he did not understand me. So I rolled up the sleeve of my coat and explained to him where we few among the group came from and who we were. Of course he had never heard of

Birkenau or persecuted Jews. I guess they did not explain to the Army that they supposedly where fighting to liberate the persecuted of Europe and that the most persecuted people in Hitler's Germany were the Jews.

Anyway, he explained to me, slowly of course, as I had asked him to, that they were the advance scouts for an American outfit, and that they had lost their way, and had no idea where their outfit was. I begged them to do something to let our three guards know that their Reich was finished and that they were not taken prisoners by our good graces. Well, he hemmed and hawed, and finally said, "Tell them to give you their submachine guns."

I think that was the proudest moment of my life, as I stepped up to the old man and said: "*Hauptscharführer*, the American officer wants your gun." I had no idea whether the American was an officer or enlisted man. I simply made him into an officer. Reluctantly, all three gave me their guns and I carried them the few steps to the vehicle. The American advised us to go on to the next town because he was sure that was where their outfit was. The country behind them was bound to be liberated by that time.

We walked on to a small town covered with white sheets hanging from every window. To this day I don't know whether the Americans had been through the town and liberated it, or whether the citizens had hung the sheets to indicate their willingness to surrender. By that time many of the prisoners who had marched with us had disappeared. Most of them had been German political prisoners anyway, so they simply walked away from the column because there were no guards left, except our three men. I remember we spent the night in a barn; we climbed up into the hay loft. The next morning the old man made sure we were all together and we went on in the direction of what he must have thought were the American lines.

We were walking on a highway, surrounded by wagons and cars among the fleeing crowd, a mix of civilians and us. Hindu's sister, Roszi, could not walk anymore. I don't remember whether her feet were bloody, or whatever was wrong with her, but we put her on a wagon and walked alongside. Suddenly we heard artillery fire, the wagon with Roszi took off, and the old man chased us off the road into the meadow and told us to run and stay together. We had been caught in a crossfire, of either Russians and Americans, or Germans and Russians, or whatever. Obviously, the War wasn't entirely over as yet, as I would find out later. We just ran following the old man.

The Blind One, (Weise) took Katja Grünberger on his back and ran with her out of harm's way. She had had polio, we assume, because she was limping and could not keep up with us. I don't remember how long we ran, across the field, and I believe it was freshly plowed, too. When we finally got away from the noise of the guns and stopped, there was a small creek running on the side of the country road that we were on. We all knelt down and drank that water; whether it was clean, where it came from, who cared? We were dehydrated with running and needed a drink.

Having refreshed ourselves, we started walking along the country lane which was completely packed by people and wagons, no cars. No one asked who we were, where we came from. All anyone was interested in was escaping the Russians. A few of us had jumped on the back of some of the wagons. People did not mind; there seemed to be a goodly amount of comradeship. I wonder how they would have felt if they knew we were Jews? But at that point I really believe they would not have cared. Suddenly there came a shout from the front somewhere out of sight: "An American checkpoint!"

We all jumped down from the various wagons and grouped together around our three guards. Walking a few minutes longer, we found ourselves stopped by a small group of soldiers with one of the strange- looking vehicles (a jeep, as we soon found out), and on the back of the jeep a man in prisoner clothing, the striped pants and jacket identifying him as a KZ survivor. We had to pass one by one in front of the soldiers who, of course, asked for identification papers. Again I could use my high school English. "Where should we go?" I asked him, as spokesperson for all of us. They had sent our three guards to a POW camp, I suppose, since they were still in their full SS uniforms. They had not even removed the insignias. "You go back from where you came" we were informed.

I rolled up my sleeve and the rest of us did as well, and said: "I don't think so: we come from Auschwitz and Ravensbrück." They just stared at us, had no idea what we were saying, but the man in the prisoner uniform, one of the liberated prisoners from the Malchow subcamp, who obviously was interpreting for them, said: "These girls were extermination camp prisoners, they have no place to go." Well, the soldiers did not quite know what to do with us since we held up the line behind us. So they said: " Go into the village ahead and ask the commanding officer of our outfit what you should do." And that is what we did. We walked the five or ten minutes on the dusty country road to the village. It was a strange feeling close to claustrophobia. This was the first time in three years that I had walked without a guard, without being told where to go, without fences or guards around me. A very strange feeling.

We stayed with the outfit in the village of Rastow in Mecklenburg District for about a week. It does sound like an incredible coincidence that I have lived for the last 35 years in Mecklenburg County in North Carolina. That is, however, historically based, since the city was named after the wife of King George III, and she happened to be a princess of Mecklenburg-Strelitz. I presume that in the meantime the CO must have made some inquiries about what to do with his uninvited guests.

At that time we got our first gentle dental check-up from an American Military Dental Unit, under the command of Dr. George I. Mills. He was nicknamed "Daddy G.I" Mills. The dentists in the group cleaned our teeth and did as much repair work as they had time to do. Obviously they were not too busy serving the outfit in the village. (Many years later I ran into George Mills while I lived in Springfield, Mo.) I presume the CO must have found a place to be rid of his guests, because one day they put us on a truck and took us to Hagenow, the district seat of the area where a former *Luftwaffe* camp had been converted into a DP -displaced persons'-camp.

The DP camp must be considered a neologism, like so many words, that have been added to the German as well as the English language since the end of the War. It was a camp to accommodate the survivors, who had no home to go to, no family that was alive anymore, no visible means of support. The Hagenow camp was, as I remember, well organized. I presume they simply kicked the *Luftwaffe* inhabitants out of it, or put them all into a POW camp, and used the well-supplied camp for the survivors. The beds in the dormitories were clean, the dining halls well equipped. The

15 of us wangled one dormitory for ourselves. It was there, I think on the first night, that I became acquainted with a young Jewish GI, Michael Kass from New York. He was clean cut, good-looking, and, what we girls immediately noticed, his uniform, like those of the other GI's, was snug over the derriere, not bagging like the German uniforms. They looked so good. I suppose this sounds terribly banal coming after years of the high drama of survival. But we were young, relatively healthy, and starved for male attention.

I remember walking with Michael on one of the camp streets and telling him about the camp. Like all the others, of course he had never heard of Birkenau. I'll never forget his words after I told him about the deprivations we all had gone through: "My Mother just complained in her last letter about not being able to get enough silk hose. Wait till I tell her how well off and lucky she has been," he said.

A few days later, when we were all in the dorm room, it must have been after breakfast, some American officers came into the room. They were looking for former SS-matrons who presumably had stripped off their uniforms and were trying to hide among the surviving prisoners in civilian clothing. The officers asked if anyone of us spoke English. I spoke up as usual, and gave them the desired information, that in our room there was no former matron. We would have known because we were all "low numbers" meaning we had all been in Birkenau for two years and more.

One of the officers asked me whether I would like a job as an interpreter with their outfit. They were the CIC (counter intelligence) group in Hagenow and needed interpreters for their interrogations. Actually, they did not really need them because the majority of them were former German refugees. They just did not want the captured Germans to know that they understood the language in case one of them would come out with something to the interpreter that they would not want known. I, of course, agreed delightedly because though there was no salary involved, I would be given a room in the HQ, and would eat in the officer's mess. That was the first time in three years that I had a private bedroom.

My work was really not very strenuous. We would drive to the small neighboring villages around Hagenow and try to find some non—Nazi party member with some standing to install as mayor of the village after deposing the faithful former Nazi mayor. And frequently we would see some young man in civilian clothing whom we would ask for his papers, and he would furtively show an ID. But then one of our officers would grab his left arm and roll up the sleeve of his shirt, and many times there would be a fresh scar on the underside of his upper arm, a vain attempt to cut out the SS tattoo identifying their blood type, together with the SS runes, that all SS members had to have tattooed on their left underarm

One evening, in the HQ mess, when we were sitting together after supper, the conversation turned to the past. One of the officers, and I am ashamed to say, I forgot his name, was a short, rather round young man, who seemed somehow familiar. He was from Berlin. As I have already indicated I had lived in Berlin for quite a while, from 1929 to 1936, and my parents had had a large circle of very good friends. On a hunch I asked the young man: "I know there were a large number of Jews in pre-war Berlin. Just by chance did you know anyone in Berlin with the name of Schürmann?"

He looked at me strangely and answered: "I sure did. Do you mean Jules Schürmann, or Louis Schürmann: they are my cousins."

"In that case," I said, "did you at either house ever meet a Mr. or Mrs. Eckstein?"

"Sure," he answered. " I played bridge with both of them. Mr. Eckstein is in Brussels, but his wife and child went to the camps. They are probably dead."

Now it was my turn to amaze him: "Mrs. Eckstein is dead, but the child is right here." It was a strange moment. He, of course, immediately through the APO (Army Post

Office), wired his cousin Louis, in London; Louis wired my uncle in New York, and my uncle wired my father, who was still in Brussels. That was one of the miracles that brought me to where I am today. Without finding my father alive I would not have known where to go. I might have ended up in Israel with a totally different fate.

I was, of course, overjoyed about that information, but come to think of it, I did not get in touch with my father directly until about July or August of 1945, shortly before I went to Brussels. I don't know if it was a matter of not having a phone number or whether the civilian phone connections between Germany and Belgium were not functioning. I really can't remember. I only know, that when I got on the train in Aachen to join my father, I had the address in Brussels: rue Vandenbussche 45, Brussels-Schaarbek. When the British took over the zone where Hagenow was located, probably somewhere around the end of May or beginning of June, 1945, I was handed over to the 521 Mil.Gov.Det (Military Government Detachment) as interpreter and moved with them from Hagenow to a small town near Aachen.

In July of 1945 I received permission to enter Belgium and took the train to Brussels. With my schoolgirl French I managed to find the right trolley car and get out at the right stop, Avenue Tervueren, and found the apartment house where my father lived, in the rue Vandenbussche, went up the stairs, and rang the bell. He opened the door. He had not changed at all.

It was an emotional reunion; I think we both cried. It had been almost 6 years since he had left Prague and since both of our lives had taken frightful as well as miraculous turns, that kept us both alive. But living there was also his mistress, Nadja Bolotine, a beautiful Russian dancer. That, of course, changed the equation somewhat as there really was not much room in the small apartment on the rue Vandenbussche and a daughter who was not much younger than the mistress must have created an awkward situation.

But we all settled in as well as possible and I began working part time for a business acquaintance of Father's as a secretary. Then I found a job as typist with the American Graves Registration where I met my first husband, Bernie Fishman. I actually met him at the G.I. Joe Ardennes Club close to the *Gare du Nord* in the Center of Brussels. I had gone downstairs in the club, because there was dancing upstairs, swing and jive, dances I did not know, and I did not have the sharp clothes that the Belgian girls had. I just was very much an outsider. So as not to look like I was glued to the wall like a wallflower, I went downstairs, and there was Bernie Fishman, looking for someone to play ping pong with. He was quite handsome in his civilian Army uniform that was almost like an officer's uniform, and he was attentive, and I was probably starved for attention. Besides I had noticed that Nadja was not very happy with my presence, though she did her best. When he asked me to marry him, eight months later, I said yes immediately. Frankly I did not think anyone would ever marry me after being in camp. I never saw myself as attractive or beautiful. On the contrary, I think I was grateful that he wanted to marry me. I later found out that like so many enticing tales of American wealth, Bernie's tale of his family was just wishful memories. My uncle had let my father know that his inquiries into the family background had produced pitiful results, but I presume, my father must have felt pressure from Nadja, or feared losing her, and so he never told me about what actually awaited me in Alton, Illinois. Bernie and I were married in Brussels in March of 1946, and that is how I came to America. The sad thing was that due to lack of money, once I was in America, I was never able to see my father again. He died in 1950 as a result of arterial sclerosis, Thus, he was indirectly also a victim of the Hitler regime.

Chapter Twelve
Coming to America

I arrived in America on July 4, 1946, with my then husband, married and pregnant. My aunt Paula, Mother's older sister, greeted us at the pier. She lived at the time on Seaman Ave. in Washington Heights across the Harlem River from Yankee Stadium. It was at that time a "good neighborhood."

My uncle had just died a few weeks before, and Paula was of course in deep mourning. It had been a good marriage; they had built a thriving business together and became quite wealthy in the process. Mother had always been envious of Paula. I still believe one of the reasons that she did not want to leave Europe when the getting was still good was that she was afraid she would have to pay the "*Reichsfluchtsteuer*," the "flight" tax, that all Jews who wanted to emigrate, had to pay, which was, according to the testimony of a number of Jews who managed to escape from the Reich, an exorbitant amount often involving the selling of one's house and other property (See p. 31, f. 1). Since it was a large percentage of everything we owned, and Mother did not want to part with anything, she lost everything and her life to boot as a result of that decision.

My favorite cousin, Hanna, Paula's only child, was there to greet me also. She had married at an early age and had already two children. She and her sister, Ruth, lived around the corner from Paula. Paula still went to the office and Hanna's husband, and Alfred, Ruth's husband, worked in the "Reproducta," the greeting card firm Siegfried had founded. Ruth, as I have previously mentioned, was uncle Siegfried's child from his first marriage; her Mother had died very young.

I arrived already pregnant with my first child and the first thing Paula did was take me to Lord and Taylor to buy me some maternity clothes. Paula offered my husband a job in the business, and God knows what our lives would have been if he had accepted. But he insisted on going "home" to Alton, Illinois, a rather God-forsaken little place outside of St Louis, Missouri.

I don't want to dwell on the details of my first marriage. Suffice it to say, I had three beautiful children altogether (The first, Jackie, was born in Decatur, Ill. My son, Todd and younger daughter, Wendy, in Springfield, Mo.). In Decatur, I had met a Viennese woman, Sofie Schlosser, who became my very good friend. She immediately advised my husband to sign up for the GI Bill of Rights and enroll in college, but my father-in-law insisted that his son had to come home to work in a shoe store where he had worked before. The obedient son obeyed. He was basically a studious type, no business acumen whatsoever, and would have become an excellent teacher, even at a university, if he would have wanted. But there was something in him that dared not contradict his father, and father was very disdainful of "eggheads," so the son could not possibly become something better than the father.

As I began to realize rather soon, that was an unusual attitude of Jewish immigrant parents in the USA. Normally they all wanted their children to "become" something. But not my husband's father. He tried to keep his sons below mediocre, so he could be the all-knowing patriarch. I finally divorced Bernie after three children—each born eight years apart-- continuous poverty, and two years of psychological counseling.

I started college at Southwest Missouri State College in Springfield, Mo., as a freshman in 1964, at the age of forty-two, when my youngest was a year old and thanks to a benefactor, whose name I don't know to this day, I was recommended for a Woodrow Wilson fellowship for graduate studies after I'd graduated in 1968. I had been already resigned to the fact that I was going to teach German and French in high school when the fellowship came along. With the help of the first black faculty member at SMS, whose name I only remember as "Mack," I wrote my proposal on why I considered foreign languages important. That was the time of the Sputnik phenomenon, and learning a foreign language for Americans was taken seriously.

The proposal was accepted and I was invited for an interview, at Kansas City. I had no money to travel there and to stay overnight for the interview. But my good friend from the Theater department (I was taking courses and appearing in plays at the Drama department, because I had to fill hours for French and German beginning courses the school had waived.), Roger, one of my gay friends, offered to drive me up in his little MG and have me stay with his mother so I could go to the interview the next morning. I remember we went to a gay nightclub that evening because Roger insisted I needed to relax. It really was fun.

The next morning at the interview, luck intervened again. One of the interviewers was a professor of German from Chicago, Franz

Heller. I was startled as he introduced himself, because my cousin George had had a very good friend in Vienna named Franzi Heller. As it turned out, this professor was the same Franzi Heller. Though I am almost sure that my German literary knowledge was not the best, I got the fellowship, and I wonder whether Franzi had something to do with it. So I packed up my few belongings, my kids, and our cat (we had to give away the dog, Putzi, and quite a few tears were shed about that), and in my old, old black Volkswagen we traveled to Lawrence, Kansas, where I had been accepted in the German Department as a graduate student.

For the first time in many years I felt almost secure. (Besides the $200.00 monthly child support I received from my former husband and my aunt's monthly contribution of $100.00, the Social Security money, which she did not need at all, I had $ 2000 per semester stipend as well as funds for books and tuition). I felt like Croesus. I remember I went to a quality clothing store in Lawrence and bought a dark blue Jersey three piece pantsuit, practically the first new thing I had bought for many years. Most of my clothes had come from my cousin Hanna, the one that changed wardrobes twice yearly. I never minded her hand-me-downs. They ranged from Armani to Valentino. At least I could look good, in spite of no money. The hand-me-down wardrobe did keep my morale up. And now I had money, a scholarship, a little two-bedroom apartment close to the university, and two years of income assured. I never worried about not keeping up my grades. That was a given.

The children were, of course, an important responsibility. Jackie, my oldest, was by that time 23, and finishing her last year at Southwest Missouri State College in Springfield. She had her own life well in hand, it seemed. I enrolled Wendy, my youngest, in the first grade in the nearby grade school. At that time children went to the closest school, and Todd, the middle child, was enrolled in high school, probably a bit farther from our apartment. Wendy could walk to school. At that time even first graders could walk by themselves. It was a safer time. Todd was a bit difficult; he was the middle child, who resented the divorce most. Jackie was too big and Wendy too little to care, but Todd felt it. I never talked with him about it, but I believe that was the root of a lot of problems in his later life.

Otherwise, the time in Lawrence was probably one of my happiest since coming to America. I made good friends, and went to lots of fun parties. I was just one of the group. In graduate school age did not seem to be a determining factor in forming circles. I was accepted, drank with the best, danced with the fastest, and smoked my bit of pot, though I found it a bit ridiculous and ineffective. At that time Senator Proxmire, from Wisconsin had initiated a "Golden Finger Award" for the most outrageously useless research grant awarded. He had just awarded a grant that supported research about the theory that red wine had histamines that cause allergies. Whoever gave that award could have just as well have given it to all graduate students who drank Gallo's Dago

Red and who would suffer from histamine allergies after a party where that beverage was the preferred brand.

My studies had to take precedent above everything since I had to maintain a high grade average for the fellowship. That did not present too much of a problem, except for writing papers, which I had to do at night, after the kids were asleep. My trusted Olympia portable had to do all the work, until my first paycheck in Charlotte, NC allowed me to buy an electric typewriter with an eraser ribbon. Anyone who has ever written a paper or a dissertation on a portable manual typewriter will remember the agony of "snipping and pasting" by hand. That was the period of the late 60's: student unrest and Kent State. K.U. had its share and I remember walking on the darkened streets, the lights having been shot out by the National Guard, and being stopped by Guardsmen and sort of interrogated.

That was also the time of my personal folly. I married a man 20 years younger than I.

Frankly there was a lot of sexual motivation behind that. He was conventional enough, I suppose, being a Turkish Jew, on insisting that we should get married; it was the right thing to do if we loved each other. Frankly I did not want to lose a satisfying affair, and so I agreed. It was a rather irresponsible thing to do, considering my children. The whole marriage only lasted until taking care of him--and he was good at letting himself be taken care of--interfered with my research on my dissertation. Then he had to go. The divorce was for free. There must have been a law in Kansas that allowed indigents-- and we were indigent God knows--to get a divorce without lawyers, only court costs.

In 1971 I had decided on a topic for my dissertation. I had thought about writing about Arthur Schnitzler, one of my favorite German authors, but my advisor, then Doctor "Mother" Ruth Angress neé Klüger, the now well- known author of Holocaust memoirs, called "*weiter leben,*" persuaded me to combine my knowledge of the Holocaust and the by-then existing

German literature about the Holocaust as a topic. The dissertation was published and had two editions. Obviously Ruth was right with her suggestion. My book on Schnitzler would have never made it to two editions. The book was published by Peter Lang Publishers in their American University Studies Edition. It's title is German Holocaust Literature, and I've even cited it in this book!

In the winter of 1972 I went to Chicago, to the annual MLA (Modern Language Association) meeting, the so-called "Slave Market." When I had started my graduate studies in 1969, language PhD's were much in demand at the universities. By 1971 the flower-children impact on the university curriculum had become so imperative that courses had to be "relevant." Courses such as history, geography, or languages were just not "relevant" anymore. Language requirements, together with many other established requirements, were dropped, and therefore I had to consider myself very lucky that the University of North Carolina at Charlotte,

(UNCC) was looking for a German language teacher with a French minor. I got the job. I moved to Charlotte in 1972 and have lived here ever since. My three children have all at one point settled in Charlotte, and since the death of my beloved third husband, Hardy Spatz, the only true love of my life, have been a great comfort to me. At least I am one of the few survivors of the Holocaust who is still surrounded by her family.

It would appear that I survived the Holocaust unscathed and picked up my life without any lasting after-effects. Physically, that is true, because somehow I have retained my physical health so far, but there are many scars that remain in my psyche that I will never get over. I have become very aggressive, or perhaps assertive, in my dealings with other people if I feel that I am being put at a disadvantage in a situation. My children think that is just my nature, and that I am just a "rude" person, as my granddaughter termed me when I did not let her inhibit me in dealing with her. I believe that I cannot let anyone know that I feel inhibited and put down and plain scared when confronted with any kind of authority. I still cringe when I am being pulled over by a traffic cop. I get nervous when I have to deal with any government official. I am afraid of being ill because illness in camp meant selection to die. Therefore, I have turned almost into a hypochondriac. I cannot stand being hungry. I get absolutely physically ill, if I experience the slightest hunger pangs.

These feelings may be hard to understand for the average American, but the hunger I experienced is not comparable to the feeling that a normal person experiences. The normal person, when feeling hungry, usually could be said to have a desire for certain foods, or food in general. When we starved the way we starved in my first four months in the outside work detail, it was the total absence of food that caused the hunger, a calculated starvation, that was meant to lead to our being ready for the gas.

People ask me what my thoughts were in Birkenau when I first entered it. It is hard to explain to a person living in today's world that one did not have the luxury of thinking in those circumstances. If we had decided to live, our entire day was taken up with thinking of survival, of avoiding anything that threatened us, of course with the exception of the selections, over which we had no control, twice daily. We had to be alert like wild animals. Wild animals don't do much thinking; they survive. That is what the newly arrived prisoner did in Birkenau.

There is of course a recurring question: "Did your faith strengthen during the camp? How did you deal with your faith?" I did not deal with my faith; I had no time for the first four months or so to even think of faith. If anyone tells me that they kept the Sabbath in the new arrival block, or kept the High Holidays, I will tell them to their face that they suffer from selective memory, which forbids them to deny any loss of faith. How would one pray to a God who watches human beings being starved and dehumanized to be ready to suffocate in a gas-filled chamber and to be burned in an oven?

Saul Friedländer, in his already cited book, The Jews in European History (See p. 208) stated that during the Holocaust God averted his face from mankind. After the Holocaust he returned to mankind. That I can accept and that I can deal with. And so I have a certain amount of my faith back. It is filled with skepticism most of the time, but I can go to the synagogue and enjoy a traditional reform service. The familiar prayers relax me and bring me a modicum of peace. Whenever I go on a trip, or before a serious decision or event, I go to services. Is it more tradition, in memory of my father's faith, or is it the comfort of old habits? I do doubt the existence of a loving and protecting God; he failed me. I can only hope that there is something left that will protect my children, but is there?

Glossary

Anschluss. Hitler's annexation of Austria in 1938. This resulted in the rapid change of the status of the Jewish community.

Appellplatz. Parade ground.

Arbeitsdienstführer. The official in charge of labor assignments in the concentration camps.

Arbeitseinsatz. The labor assignment office.

Aufbaukommando. Jewish Construction pioneer transport from Prague to Theresienstadt (AK I and AK II), which prepared Theresienstadt for the Jewish deportees.

Aufseherin. A matron in charge of women prisoners.

Aussenkommandos. Outside work detail. These were the most exhausting jobs in Birkenau demanding heavy physical labor from the prisoners with minimal tools. Normally, in two months most of those in the Aussenkommando would either be dead or ready for "the gas."

Bauleitung. Construction department

Blockführer. SS-man or matron, responsible for a block.

blockovas (Czech). Prisoners in charge of blocks. They were responsible for distributing the food and keeping order in each of the women's blocks. They had been recruited among the Jewish women who were first brought to the camp in 1942.

Effektenkammer. Clothing department.

Effektenspezialisten. Experts in the warehousing of the prisoners' clothing.

Familienlager. The "family camp" set up in Auschwitz in September, 1943 as a "back up" to the phony "Embellishment" in Theresienstadt to impress the Red Cross of the "Humanitarian" treatment of the Jews by the Nazis. The camp was liquidated in March, 1944; all but 100 of the 5600 men and women and children in the camp were killed in the gas chambers.

Freizeitgestaltung. Leisure Time Department established in Theresienstadt that arranged cabarets, various other performances and even operas presented by the many talented prisoners in the camp.

"geschleust." past tense of "schleusen" Theresienstadt slang for taking the property from arriving transports. "To liberate" would be equivalent English in World War II slang.
Hauptscharführer. SS equivalent of First Sergeant.

Judenälteste, head of the *Judenrat,* Council of Elders that was established by the Nazis as "representative" groups of prominent members of the Jewish community. They were used as a cover to carry out Nazi policies, especially in terms of making up lists for deportation.

Jugendlager. A camp which contained one gas chamber for a number of people to be exterminated.

Kanada. The work detail that sorted and stored all of the possessions that had been confiscated from the prisoners on entering Auschwitz-Birkenau. Also the storehouse itself.

Kapo. Mostly German or Polish criminals or political prisoners, who had been made the foreperson of a work detail, male or female.

Kasernen. German translation of barracks

Kleiderkammer. The place where all the Aryan prisoners' clothing was kept.

Koje. Bunks These were the beds that the women in Birkenau slept in. It was ironically named since it also described a state room on a cruise ship.

Kommando. Generic name for the work-details in Birkenau.

Krankenbau. The hospital bloc in Birkenau.

kumbal (Czech). A private room that was often built in the large vaults or in the stair-wells of the fortress of Theresienstadt.

Lager. Generic name for a concentration camp

Lagersperre. Curfew.

Läuferin. This was a liaison runner between offices in the camps. There were no telephones.

Luftwaffe. German air force.

Mischling. A person of half-Jewish "blood." Treated less villainously by the Nazis than full-blooded Jews.

Muselmann. A person who has lost the will to live as a result of his or her treatment in the camps. A Zombie (Literally a "Muslim.").

Obersturmführer. SS term for first lieutenant.

Politische Abteilung. Literally Political Department, but actually the Gestapo headquarters.

Prominente. Important members of the Jewish community that were given "special" treatment in Theresienstadt. Although their living quarters were better than those of other prisoners, they also suffered the same terrible conditions.

Rapportschreiberin (recording secretary) highest ranking Jewish prisoner in the woman's camp.

Reichfluchtsteuer. The excessive tax Jews had to pay--25% of their net worth or earnings-- in order for them to be allowed to emigrate. This tax was actually instituted in 1931 before the Nazi take-over of Germany.

Rotkäppchen. "Little Red Riding Hood," the ironic name given to the *Kanada* work detail.

Rottenführer. SS term for corporal.

Schreibstube. The administrative headquarters of the women's camp in Auschwitz-Birkenau.

Schutzhäftling. "Protective custody" prisoner. The Nazi euphemism for the Jews who were designated for extermination.

Sonderkommando. The work detail whose responsibility it was to take the corpses from the gas chambers to be incinerated.

Stabsgebäude. Staff building of Auschwitz-Birkenau.

Standesamt. The ironically named bridal registry office; the large office, where every death in the camp was recorded.

Strafkommando. The punishment detail in which prisoners who had been found guilty of a camp rule infraction were worked extremely hard.

Stubenälteste. Theresienstadt equivalent of "blockova" in Birkenau.

stubovas. (Czech). Cleaning and maintenance personnel in the women's blocs.

Transporthilfe. The transport assistance detail which brought the luggage to the Fairgrounds Palace in Prague where the transports collected.

Umschlagplatz. The point of departure for the Jews who were being deported to the camps.

Unterscharführer. SS term for non-commissioned officer.

Untersturmführer. SS term for second lieutenant.

Vernichtungslager. Extermination camp

Weisskäppchen. Rag-picking detail

Zählappell. Roll-call. The prisoners would have to stand for hours while their numbers were called in order to keep track of who was still alive.

Zeichenstube. The graphics department.

Zulage. Extra rations given to some prisoners on special occasions.

277
Index

278